Group Activities for Social Emotional Learning using Sketch Comedy and Improv Games

GROUP ACTIVITIES FOR SOCIAL EMOTIONAL LEARNING USING SKETCH COMEDY AND IMPROV GAMES

Shawn Amador, LCSW and
Eleni S. Liossis, PsyD, ATR, RDT

Jessica Kingsley Publishers
London and Philadelphia

First published in Great Britain in 2023 by Jessica Kingsley Publishers
An imprint of Hodder & Stoughton Ltd
An Hachette Company

2

Copyright © Shawn Amador, LCSW & Eleni S. Liossis, PsyD, ATR, RDT 2023

The right of Shawn Amador, LCSW & Eleni S. Liossis, PsyD, ATR, RDT
to be identified as the Author of the Work has been asserted by them in
accordance with the Copyright, Designs and Patents Act 1988.

Front cover image source: 123RF. The cover image is for illustrative
purposes only, and any person featuring is a model.

All pages marked with ✳ can be downloaded at https://library.jkp.com/
redeem for personal use with this program, but may not be reproduced for
any other purposes without the permission of the publisher.

A CIP catalogue record for this title is available from the British Library and the Library of Congress

ISBN 978 1 83997 292 8
eISBN 978 1 83997 293 5

Printed and bound by CPI Group (UK) Ltd, Croydon, CR0 4YY

Jessica Kingsley Publishers' policy is to use papers that are natural, renewable, and recyclable
products and made from wood grown in sustainable forests. The logging and manufacturing
processes are expected to conform to the environmental regulations of the country of origin.

Jessica Kingsley Publishers
Carmelite House
50 Victoria Embankment
London EC4Y 0DZ

www.jkp.com

CONTENTS

PREFACE

As a school social worker, co-author Shawn sought to find ways for her students to have their voices heard and practice social emotional skills. In combining a passion for clowning and the need for fun social emotional learning, a clown troupe was started in Shawn's school, which morphed into a social emotional skills sketch comedy troupe called Social Theatre™. Shawn's creative programming with the use of clowning and social emotional learning earned her the Heartspring Award for Innovation and Creativity in Special Education. Shawn has presented at multiple conferences across the US including the Social Thinking Providers Conference, Illinois School Social Workers Conference, the Yes... and Mental Health Conference, and the Learning and the Brain Conference. Now, Social Theatre™ is utilized for group therapy in a clinic setting as well as in schools. Having worked in schools for 20 years, Shawn is now practicing as a full-time therapist in private practice where she runs Social Theatre™ groups. Moreover, Shawn continues to develop programming and is now teaching at university level where she is utilizing Improv games and active learning activities to teach concepts in the Social Work program at Concordia University Chicago.

In these groups, some plays have been written which are included in this book. Both parents and Social Theatre™ participants have given consent to share the plays they have helped write, so that others can utilize them for social emotional learning. Moreover, publishing the plays is a way to help those involved in Social Theatre™ to feel that they have a voice and to know that the topics and lessons they wrote about are making a difference in the world. To this day, Social Theatre™'s website publishes participants' written plays to continue original contributions on socialtheatre.org.

Dr. Eleni S. Liossis, PsyD, ATR, RDT, is a licensed clinical psychologist, registered art therapist and registered drama therapist. Some of her certifications include Social Thinking® and working with neurodiverse populations. Along with her clinical training, Dr. Liossis is a Second City trained comedy actor. Her program *ModProv*, applies expressive arts and drama/Improv techniques for clinical application in therapeutic and school settings. Dr. Liossis also has a private practice, *Happy Human LLC*.

All worksheet pages marked with a ✷ can be photocopied or downloaded from https://library.jkp.com/redeem using the code EBPSKLR

ACKNOWLEDGMENTS

SA: I would like to acknowledge the Social Theatre™ participants by saying how amazing and wonderful you are, and hope you find that your exploration, discovery and practice of these social skills concepts which have become activities and plays will help many others in their exploration. Having been through the process of brainstorming, collaborative idea building, accepting each other's ideas, performance, and now in a published book, you have every reason to be proud! Each and every one of you are talented and can do so much in this world! To the parents, community members, and colleagues at CORE Connection: your feedback has been inspiring, and your support and enthusiasm and involvement along this journey have been much appreciated! :) I would also like to acknowledge my brother, Jeremy Heerdt, for his amazing creativity and help with the website, as well as my parents, husband, and children for their never-ending support and love.

EL: Thank you to my parents, husband, and children for their amazing love and support. A very special thanks to my wonderful kids for their inspiration. Great appreciation and thanks to my patients, students, colleagues, and friends who supported me on this journey. Thank you to Shawn, for the opportunity to collaborate on this book.

Chapter 1

HISTORY OF SOCIAL THEATRE, RESEARCH, AND METHODOLOGY

HISTORY OF SOCIAL THEATRE™

Social Theatre™ began as an afterschool clown troupe program on the southwest side of Chicago. Since then, the program has transitioned into a sketch comedy Improv troupe called Social Theatre™. Social Theatre™ has also been utilized as a group therapy program in the clinical setting, with children dealing with anxiety and social deficits.

Since Social Theatre™ is an evolving program, it is important to learn more about the roots of the program and participant viewpoints. An ethnographic study was conducted in the school program, where participants described the clown program as having components of "stress relief," "humor," "teamwork," and "role modeling." Moreover, participants reported that they were able to "teach what we learn." In Shawn Amador's first book, *Teaching Social Skills through Sketch Comedy and Improv Games*, a collaborative script development process for participants to write original material was discussed in detail. Although the clown program has morphed into sketch comedy, Social Theatre™ continues to have the same mission and purpose: to actively learn social skills and teach them to others.

As for this book, we are providing targeted social skill-based Improv games, participant-written plays, and basic plays that are meant to be added onto. To increase participant comfort levels with Improv and sketch comedy, this book includes a graduated exposure of techniques, starting with Improv trust building and joint focus games. Then we slowly build complexity through Improvisation and role playing, which then fosters writing sketches and scripts.

OTHER APPLICATIONS OF SOCIAL THEATRE™

Social Theatre™ techniques can be utilized throughout the school day, as well as in afterschool programs and in group therapy settings. During the school day, the activities can be applied in classroom groups, such as intervention groups for writing and/or social skills. As referenced in the first book (Amador, 2018) school-wide playwriting contests can provide a myriad of academic and social emotional benefits, as students can form a short-term group to develop a play with the help of the theatre troupe or group leader. Social Theatre™ strategies and plays can be utilized in afterschool programs, where students can practice and perform original plays about social skills for the school and/or community. In the therapy setting, Social Theatre™ plays and social skill Improv can be utilized to teach deeper therapeutic concepts.

Utilizing books and worksheets to teach social skills is helpful as well, however it is essential to follow up with the practice of the skills/role plays or activities. These programs are essential in boosting confidence while providing opportunities to enhance interpersonal communications. Research, discussed below, shows that theatre and improvisation can help bridge this gap. Specifically, studies show benefits in collaboration, improvisation, and theatre are effective in increasing social skills, imagination, coping skills, and academic skills.

RESEARCH AND METHODOLOGY

When engaging students in writing literature, many factors come into play. The key factors are: having trust between participants, having the courage to share ideas, and accepting healthy criticism. When the collaborative factor is added, the skills of being able to give encouragement, accept and build on others' ideas, and being able to integrate or move on from one's own ideas become essential.

With the use of this book, educators and therapists will be able to lead their participants through the process of learning social skills and collaboration skills, in "real time"—all while further opening the doors to creativity. Moreover, participants will be increasing their trust in their own ideas, as well as trust in themselves, in being more vulnerable through practice and performance. Through the process of idea sharing, participants will have opportunities to show acceptance and build upon others' ideas.

Utilizing improvisational theatre is trending in current research. In DeMichelle's 2015 study, dramatic increases in writing amounts were shown when comparing the traditional language arts classroom to a language arts class with Improv. For those who had 504 plans and Individualized Education Programs (IEPs), a 310 percent increase in writing was noted.

The results are believed to be due to the basic rules of Improv, which provide a more emotionally safe environment and a general acceptance of all ideas that can also be built upon. Recently, Mary DeMichelle was able to explore reasons why Improv is so effective in a study of 32 subjects between the ages of 15 and 18 who had met the criteria for complex developmental trauma. In pre- and post-qEEG brain scans, DeMichelle and Kuenneke (2021) found that parts of the brain which were inaccessible due to trauma had been reactivated with the use of 20 minutes of short-form Improv. The speed of neuroconnections, along with the ability to access parts of the brain which make sense of non-verbal and verbal communication, were at optimal levels. This allowed neuroconnections to be made with the left brain, which is often inaccessible or has limited access after complex developmental trauma.

Within the general neurodiverse population, who may or may not have had exposure to developmental trauma, but may have difficulties in social situations, social contact can be traumatizing. Dr. Van Der Kolk (2014) states that humans can also have "mini-traumas" which can impact feelings of safety and can also cause fight or flight reactions. Incorporating and modifying Improv in different settings and with differing abilities, as well as helping participants through practicing of plays, allows opportunity for social connection, a safe place to make mistakes and feel accepted. With the use of sketches, participants are able to put into plays their own ideas, as well as practice simple, unscripted role plays. Practicing plays unscripted, as well as the use of Improv, can give needed exposure to spontaneity as well as uncertainty. Felsman and colleagues (2020) studied the effects of Improv versus regular socialization and found that Improv increased problem solving as well as better acceptance of uncertainty. The authors discuss that many forms of mental illness stem from intolerance of uncertainty. Populations that Social Theatre™ has been utilized with, including those with Autism, anxiety and ADHD, can have difficulty with not knowing details and accepting changes.

Research shows that Improv techniques support decreases in anxiety, specifically "trait anxiety." A study applying an Improv program called SENSE Theatre, run in coordination with Vanderbilt University (Corbett *et al.,* 2016), demonstrated that Improv with neurotypical peers, children and teens on the spectrum demonstrated a decrease in their outward anxiety signs and spent more time in group play after the intervention. More specifically for those diagnosed with ASD, there was a decrease in anxiety signs after the intervention, as well as an increase of time spent interacting with peers. However, it was reported that before these participants were in treatment, their outward anxiety had increased during unstructured play sessions.

In comparison, this study looked at effects of anxiety after a ten-week Improv class in a classroom setting. In the Felsman and colleagues (2019) study, 43 percent of participants were measured to have a social phobia before the intervention, whereas zero participants measured to have a social phobia post-intervention. Corbett and colleagues (2016) discuss how anxiety appears to decrease as it correlates with increasing social skills. Similarly, Felsman's study finds that participants significantly rated themselves as having better social skills after the ten-week Improv intervention.

Most recently, Felsman and colleagues (2020) compared socialization benefits after 20 minutes of Improv. It was found that 20 minutes of Improv increased positive affect, problem solving exploration, and promoted acceptance of uncertainty. The researchers explained many forms of mental health difficulties occur because of difficulty with uncertainty; however, Improv offers exposure to uncertainty but within a supportive and fun environment.

In Corbett and colleagues' 2017 study, significant social skills improvements were found. The study measured facial recognition, perspective taking, theory of mind skills, and group play across environments. While on the waitlist, the future participants were utilized as the control group. Assessments were utilized for the waitlist control group and the experimental group. The experimental group included an Improvisational class for youth with ASD alongside neurotypical peers. Unstructured play opportunities were available before and after the group. The amount of play that group members participated in was measured. The study measured significant differences between the experimental group and waitlist control group, as skills were increased in the areas of facial recognition, perspective taking and theory of mind skills, and group play across environments.

The studies below consider brain chemistry in relation to social connection and experiencing fun together. It has been found that fun and social connection advances self-esteem, memory, motivation, learning, and stress tolerance.

In an article titled "The psychology of belonging", Myra Laldin (2016) discussed how the brain reacts when someone feels left out. Levels of cortisol, also referred to as the stress hormone, increase. When cortisol increases in the brain, the cognitive process that allows higher level thinking is blocked. Thus, the feeling of belonging is essential in learning environments.

Siegel and Bryson (2012) discuss the brain's chemistry during fun and play. These authors state that dopamine is released when people are having fun, which also provides greater self-esteem and stress tolerance. Hamid and colleagues (2016) studied dopamine release in connection with work and motivation. They found that dopamine release was directly correlated to work motivation. Singh Bains and colleagues (2014) found that showing humorous videos to the older populations increased memory, recall, and the learning process.

Vera and colleagues (2012) studied a large survey sample of high school students. They asked questions about life's difficulties, signs of depression, and coping skills. For those who had signs of depression and/or bigger life difficulties, the most significant and effective coping skill was humor.

Stephen Porges (2017) discussed the components of the Polyvagal Theory, which defines physiological states. When in a calm state, we can recognize cues in our environment such as others' feelings, body language and voice tones. However, in heightened states, our brain misinterprets cues as well as makes us feel unsafe, which is also known as the fight or flight state. Thus, social cue recognition can be hindered when in the fight or flight state, versus being in a calm state will allow one to recognize social cues. Furthermore, the neuro-response to laughter is the increase in feelgood chemicals including dopamine and serotonin (Edwards, 2010). The collaborative humor of Social Theatre™ provides opportunities for social connectedness, while the third-person approach provides a feeling of safety. For example, Social Theatre™ participants work on understanding social situations and social skills through exaggerating, practicing, and seeing third-person social incongruities. Moreover, in our practice of social emotional skills through short plays and Improv, we are becoming more comfortable with the idea of making social mistakes. This also expands our stress tolerance window.

HOW CAN SOCIAL THEATRE™ BE APPLIED?

Social Theatre™ is a way to make social emotional learning active. It is an opportunity for "real time" learning. In utilizing Improv and skits, participants can work on socialization skills, while also having fun. Due to the nature of Improv and sketch comedy, the process includes engaging activities or third-person stories. Therefore, concepts and skills can be ingested without personalization.

SOCIAL EMOTIONAL LEARNING AND PARTS OF IMPROV

On David Letterman's show, "My Next Guest Needs No Introduction" (2018), Tina Fey discusses the rules of Improv as adding ideas with sentences, accepting ideas by saying "Yes, and...", as well as knowing there are no mistakes. When Improvising with others, it is important to accept their ideas and build onto the story with more details. Moreover, it is also important to be able to see mistakes as an opportunity. Mistakes often happen in Improv when someone misinterprets our actions, but we must be flexible in being able to accept the statement of our Improv partners as the story.

Viola Spolin talks about the "Seven Aspects of Spontaneity" in her book, *Improvisation for the Theater* (1999). In the first one, Games, she states that games provide a natural group form in which personal freedom is necessary for the experience. Spolin (1999) adds that Games develop the skills necessary for the game itself, through play. Followed by the skills being developed during this time, the person is having fun playing the game, which in turn is the exact moment the person is truly open to receive the offers from the game (Spolin, 1999). Spolin goes further in saying: "Any game worth playing is highly social and has a problem that needs solving within it – an objective point in which each individual must become involved..." (Spolin, 1999, p. 5). This highlights the importance of developing and making social connections, through the game play process in theatre games. Applying this to using Improv or sketch comedy techniques in teaching social and emotional skills, it's clear that game play fosters this development.

In relating the rules of Improv to Social Emotional Standards, social awareness is specifically targeted with listening, recognizing situational demands and opportunities. Family and community involvement are also utilized as Social Theatre™ can be utilized from the smallest one-on-one interventions of role play to classroom work, school-wide interventions, and community performances (CASEL, 2022). Relationship skills addressed are communication, resolving conflict, collaborative problem solving, and seeking and offering support.

Utilizing improvisational theatre techniques even for a brief amount of time has been shown to be effective at decreasing anxiety and depression, while increasing self-esteem (Krueger *et al.*, 2017). As improvisational theatre includes social connection, acceptance of mistakes, fun, behavioral rehearsal, and elements of exposure therapy, it is easy to see why it helps so quickly. Utilizing Improv as a method in therapy, schools, and with kids, teens, and those with social difficulties is essential.

BUILDING SKILL-BASED ACTIVITIES FROM SCRATCH

The goal of Social Theatre™ is to turn the process of social emotional learning into an active learning experience. A couple ways to think about how to begin this process are:

1. Consider the skill you are trying to teach.

2. Find ways to break down the skill into the most basic steps or form in order to turn it into an active learning lesson that the participants will understand.

The plays will center around teaching the chosen skill but with an added conflict. In a lot of plays from Social Theatre™, the conflict comes from not utilizing the social skill correctly, but at other times plays are about competing factors, such as perspectives. In a play about perspectives, the skill would be to stop to think about the other person and try to think of what they might be thinking and feeling. Thus, it is important to think about splitting components into competing factors. The process of brainstorming the competing factors with the group can be a learning experience in itself.

When thinking about play creation, it is important to recognize the competing factors and themes that are being brought forth. The play should include one conflict in the most simplified version. Separating concepts into a play with one conflict can create a basis for a play.

The competing factors could be:

-   feelings versus actions

-   bad memories versus good memories

-   thoughts of encouragement versus thoughts of self-deprecation

-   feeling emotionally safe versus feeling emotionally unsafe

-   others' feelings versus my feelings

-   fulfilling my needs versus fulfilling others' needs

-   happy versus sad

-   hero versus villain

-   expert versus novice

-   holding on versus letting go.

When these components are separated, we can utilize Improv techniques or develop a written dialogue to have the components talk to each other. In this type of activity, we are figuring out the root of a problem or perspective—what Improv describes as "finding the stakes."

If the members of the group have been traumatized or are sensitive to a specific topic, they will benefit from more distance from reality. Sketch comedy can be utilized instead, as events and characters can be planned. To utilize sketch comedy, the traumatizing factor must be exaggerated or changed to the point of not being real. This will occur by twisting a component to incorporate something wacky. Let's take an example in which the scene is about someone feeling emotionally unsafe because they are visiting someone with a tarantula versus the other role of the person who owns the tarantula and feels safe. The object that is scary (the tarantula) can be twisted into something not scary, such as rainbows and unicorns. The fear of something that is not typically scary to anyone would in itself be humorous and more digestible.

MEANING OF HUMOR IN SOCIAL THEATRE™

As humor is a powerful coping strategy, Vera *et al.* (2012) found it to be the most effective buffer between life difficulty and signs of mental illness. Humor can give a buffer or distance from a problem, thus creating more self-protection. Thus, the emotional distance that is given to social skills learning through sketch comedy can be powerful to those who are insecure about social difficulties. Using comedy to teach can be a way to get the message across in a way that is received more easily. As Shawn has noted, Social Theatre™ is like "a spoonful of sugar that helps the medicine go down."

However, when in a group, it is important to focus on engaging in the present moment with each other, while building ideas. The humor comes naturally from being present with others. Yet, if humor is forced or someone becomes more of a stand-up comedian, it can throw off the collaborative and cohesive energy of a group.

Examples of effective humor might come from combining mismatched ideas that when singled out would not be funny. For example, this could happen with idea building during a word game, such as "Three Things", where we all take turns identifying things in a category. The category might be things you consume. The identified objects might be completely random at first, such as "cheese, Starbucks, and shoes." At times, participants will not be able to think of words, therefore are encouraged to say the first word that comes to mind, which is also accepted. When combined in a story, the words become more interesting and at times comical.

Students on the Autism spectrum can have difficulty understanding humor. In a study about humor training and Autism, Ching-Lin Wu and colleagues (2016) studied how humor training for those on the spectrum (<70 IQ) enabled participants to increase their understanding of "nonsense humor," as well as "affiliative humor." Nonsense humor is when the same word is used in a joke, but has two meanings. Affiliative humor is the ability to be in a social situation and demonstrate use of humor by laughing about occurrences that happen in everyday life.

However, some who are on the Autism spectrum can learn to understand incongruencies. In teaching about incongruencies, first start with showing pictures that are incongruent. For example, in Social Theatre™, we utilize a picture of an Ironman LEGO® statue, with a flamboyant purple wig photoshopped onto it. We then discuss why the LEGO® statue does not match with the wig. We take it further and discuss how the participants are feeling about it. Once participants gain a better understanding about incongruencies, they are then challenged further, such as by watching videos of animals acting like humans. For example, we like to show a video of the "goat screaming like a lady." We then discuss what our expectations of goats are, such as how they sound and act. However, when our ears are telling us we hear a lady screaming, the sound and behavior of the goat does not match up. This then presents a clear incongruency that can be discussed.

Social Theatre™ sets the ground rules that mismatched humor about behavior and relationships is only funny on stage or on screen. Thus, when trying to be funny off stage or even while conversing with others, one can sometimes make others feel awkward or maybe even create social distancing when the humor is not given or received as intended.

Considering adding humor to a play, it is important to understand that humor is not doing something random or without reason. For example, hitting oneself in the face with a straw repeatedly is not humor, and may even be an unsuccessful attempt to gain attention which could make others feel annoyed. To utilize this example, there would need to be a *reason* to hit oneself in the head with a straw. This could be if a person is not paying attention while trying to drink from a straw and it hits their cheek. Or a person sneezes and the straw hits their forehead. When taking this moment during a play, explain to participants that their moment needs to be exaggerated because once the action is completed, it cannot be repeated unless there is a continued reason.

GROUP HUMOR VERSUS STAND-UP COMEDY

When people think of comedy, they think of making people laugh. The purpose of Social Theatre™ is to be part of a group and have fun, which typically results in laughter. Thus, one of the major ground rules is to contribute to the group by being present and in the moment. This is done through listening to others, idea-building together, and adding one's own responses to the group as a whole. Therefore, if someone is not sharing the spotlight with others, perhaps they can be given the option to work on an individual comedy routine, outside of the group setting, in order to share in a different and supportive setting.

For some leaders that might not have the time or comfort level to create their own skill-based Improv activities, more are included in this book. For participants to be active in a group, they need to trust that the group is a safe space to take risks. Therefore, the activities in the next chapter include Improv activities that can actively teach group rules and norms.

RULES OF IMPROV FOR SOCIAL THEATRE™
GROUPS AND ACTIVITIES

For the purposes of this book, we will be combining basic Improv rules and expectations with therapeutic applications. In other words, the general and more commonly applied rules of Improv that are seen and worked with in the theatre and performance setting will be somewhat different in this context. This is to allow for the therapeutic and social/emotional applications of learning. Please refer to the worksheet opposite whenever the group is utilizing an Improv activity to remind participants about accepting others' ideas and being flexible.

RULES OF IMPROV FOR SOCIAL THEATRE™ GROUPS AND ACTIVITIES

For the purposes of this book, we will be combining basic Improv rules and expectations with therapeutic applications. In other words, the general and commonly seen rules of Improv that are applied mostly in the theatre and performance setting will be somewhat different in this context. This is to allow for the therapeutic and social/emotional applications of learning. Please note these rules should be applied to all the activities in this book. Refer to this worksheet at needed, as the rule breakdown is not repeated throughout the book. Below is the breakdown:

Rules of Improv in Social Theatre™:

All ideas are accepted.

We build on others' ideas.

Improv is to share imagination.

Expectations of Improv in Social Theatre™:

Be open and flexible, even if an idea does not fit.

Whatever is said in the scene, accept it and build on others' ideas.

Most importantly, have fun while learning!!

SUMMARY

Overviews of the history, research and applications of Social Theatre™ were discussed. We also discussed types of humor and the general rules of Improv in Social Theatre™, which are applied in all our activities. In Chapter 2, the focus will be on the structure of the groups, rules and expectations, and establishing boundaries. Activities range from learning how to participate in a group, to expectations of an audience member, and sharing the attention.

ESTABLISHING GROUP FLOW WITH BOUNDARIES AND RULES

It is very important to establish the rules of a group at the very beginning of any group project. This helps set boundaries and keep a consistent group flow. With younger groups, it provides clear expectations and supports the group leader in their work as well. The following is a breakdown of rules, structure and group flow ideas that can help groups run more smoothly.

HOW TO RUN THE SOCIAL THEATRE™ GROUP ACTIVITIES IN THIS BOOK
1: Establish and review rules of Social Theatre™

Please refer to the worksheet in Chapter 1, *Rules of Improv for Social Theatre™ Groups and Activities*.

Rules of Social Theatre™ Improv

- All ideas are accepted.

- We build on others' ideas.

- Improv is to share imagination.

Expectations of Improv in Social Theatre™

- Be open and flexible, even if an idea does not fit.

- Whatever is said in the scene, accept it and build on others' ideas.

- Most importantly, have fun while learning!!

2: Safety guidelines

To begin utilizing Social Theatre™, participants must understand that there are rules in order to keep each other safe—both emotionally and physically. It is encouraged to develop the group rules together, through brainstorming and open discussion. This process may take up one entire session, as the group needs to agree on the rules and boundaries set.

For example, the group can brainstorm their own rules through a game of charades. This is done by asking each participant to make a movement, symbolizing a rule that the group should implement. The group can then discuss why this rule is important.

Social Theatre™ rules should also include:

- No touching.

  - Even if a scene shows that someone is to be touched, a freeze will happen beforehand.

- Humor in Social Theatre™ is for the entire group.

- Everyone's ideas are accepted in Improv and brainstorming.

- If run by a therapist, personal information disclosed will be kept private, by all members.

  - In other words: what is said in group, stays in group (with the exception of when someone discloses risk of injury to self or others).

3: Establishing group flow with boundaries and rules

It is very important to establish the rules of a group at the very beginning of any group project. This helps set boundaries and keep a consistent group flow. With younger groups, it provides clear expectations and supports the group leader in their work as well. In Social Theatre™, group rules and boundaries are the same across all activities. In addition, Improv rules are also the same. This helps simplify the review process and gets the group quickly acclimatized to what the expectations are. The following chapter walks through several activities that help establish the group flow, boundaries, and rules.

4: Maintaining group flow and structure

When it comes to groups, it is vital that the leader keeps the momentum and structure going. The flow of the group helps determine the level of progress and, in turn, the structure helps keep the flow going. The following activities help establish flow and structure to your groups.

5: Materials needed and defining space

In order to create group structure and flow, materials and space can be thought out ahead of time. Materials typically needed are paper, writing tools and a dry erase board. Space needs include stage space for performances and seating for observers or audience. When running activities and Improv games in non-performance times, space for physical movement is needed.

6: Differentiation according to participant needs

The activities in this book are designed to be interactive. When a participant struggles with sharing or feels too nervous to perform, allow them to observe or play the part of the audience member only. Group participants can be encouraged to give peers ideas as well.

Rules, boundaries and routines in group are essential in trust building within groups. We also understand that participants can learn best by practicing rules through active learning exercises. The purpose of the following activities is to teach about setting rules, boundaries, and group structure through active learning.

ACTIVE LEARNING FOR ESTABLISHING RULES, STRUCTURE, AND GROUP FLOW

SILLY HANDS

Using hands in group communication

Goals

- Learn, observe, and experience the act of raising hands versus not raising hands.

- Participants will learn using patience, turn-taking, and listening skills, while also developing their self-concepts.

Materials needed

- Recommended: Use *Calm and Silly Hands Cards* (see overleaf).

Setting the purpose

To build a supportive group, it's helpful to observe and follow the rules of hand-raising. When we make connections with others, it is easier to trust each other and ultimately to work together in a group, especially in the performance of scenes.

The following skills are taught and developed in this activity:

- Listening to peers.

- Building group trust.

- Making connections with others.

- Accepting each other's choices in scenes.

Review the expected and unexpected examples of hand-raising versus not hand-raising:

- Some unexpected examples include interrupting a class or a group setting, blurting out, yelling out, or not addressing one's needs.

- Some expected examples might include (depending upon participant ability and comfort level): respecting others' time by not interrupting them, waiting patiently to be called on, speaking in turn, patiently raising their hand, and active listening. To prepare for *Silly Hands*, participants can brainstorm examples of expected and unexpected hand-raising. (Have participants also write out a list for themselves.)

  Participants can brainstorm the following examples (keep on the board for visual support):

- Times when others were expected to raise their hands.

- Times when they are not expected to raise their hands.

- Times they felt respected or disrespected.

- Times they felt genuinely listened to versus ignored.

Each group member should choose one brief example to share with the rest of the group.

Instructions for *Silly Hands*

1. One participant will become the "teacher" or "leader", per scene.

2. Scene teacher/leader will choose a simple activity that they will try to teach the rest of the group, with the help of the group leader (e.g., Improv game *Zip-Zap-Zop* (see Chapter 10) or a game of Simon Says).

3. *Silly Hands* prompt cards will then be randomly handed out, to help participants know which role to play: *silly hands or calm hands*.

4. Scene leader/teacher will be prompted to begin teaching a simple activity to the group.

5. Soon after, the group leader will prompt the participants to act out their roles and to start interacting with the "leader/teacher."

6. When the exercise is complete, discuss as a whole group how the experience was for them.

7. What parts made them feel comfortable versus uncomfortable.

8. What would they have done or felt if they were placed in a real situation where this applied?

9. Repeat the above steps until all participants have had the chance to be the leader/teacher.

CALM AND SILLY HANDS CARDS

Calm Hands

Silly Hands

Wrap up (group discussion)

- How was the experience for all participants?

- What did you notice about hand-raising?

- What happened with the hand-raising that was expected?

- What happened with hand-raising that was unexpected?

- How did the expected hand-raising make people feel?

- How did the unexpected hand-raising make people feel?

Through the whole-group discussion, process what they thought about the experience in general. Point out the general views of how unexpected behaviors make things difficult or uncomfortable.

HOT SAUCE

Non-verbal body language in group communication

Goals

- To learn, observe, and experience giving and receiving constructive criticism.

- Participants will also expand on accepting constructive criticism, giving and receiving group feedback, and practice positive social behaviors.

- In addition, they will practice acknowledging uncomfortable feelings and reactions to uncomfortable situations, along with noticing participants' uncomfortable responses.

Materials needed

- Recommended visual(s): *Hot Sauce Continuum Chart* (see following pages).

Introduction to *Hot Sauce*

In the book *Think Social: A Social Thinking® Curriculum for School Age Students* (2008) the author, Michelle Garcia Winner employs the terms "expected and unexpected behavior." This refers to behaviors that make others feel uncomfortable or comfortable. People who feel comfortable around us typically find it easier to develop a relationship with us. At times when we exhibit unexpected behaviors, such as not following the unwritten social norms, it can make others feel uncomfortable. They might misunderstand us. In turn, it is highly recommended to review specifically what behaviors are expected when one is an audience member versus performer before starting the activity. Some examples are: staying quiet during the performance, whispering versus distracting facial expressions, talking out, heckling or laughing at inappropriate times, and making rude comments.

A visual worksheet has been created to help define the different expectations of each role presented in this lesson. Here is brief breakdown of the roles:

Roles

Audience

Expected behaviors from the audience during a performance are: to listen and support with clapping, positive facial expressions, and compliments after the scene. However, when there is an unexpected behavior in a scene, the audience's role is to utilize the "hot sauce" motions to demonstrate how uncomfortable they are. This movement can range from a small motion of tasting the "hot sauce," to an extreme motion of a burning taste of "hot sauce."

Scene actors

The scene actors' job is to perform two plays, one with expected behaviors and the other with unexpected behaviors. Their job also includes understanding that they are in character, while also trying to teach a specific concept.

Below are some example scenarios that can be used by the scene actors:

- Listening with entire body (Whole Body Listening) versus not listening (moving body, eyes not on speaker).

  (Whole Body Listening involves integrating all of the body's senses, combined with using executive functioning skills (self-control of brain and body), and perspective taking (thinking of others and what they are saying). (Hendrix *et al.*, 2013))

- Reading the room: coming into a room quietly versus coming into a quiet room loudly.

- A teacher or friend is talking and the student or friend is listening versus looking at their phone.

- A teacher is teaching, students are learning versus a student trying to talk to other students during learning.

- Making all group members feel accepted versus not talking to one group member.

- Waiting in line versus running to the front to be first.

Note: examples can also be created by group participants and/or the leader.

Other applications

The *Hot Sauce Continuum* can also be utilized when a group member feels uncomfortable. Participants can actually work on matching their level of discomfort to the level of discomfort on the *Hot Sauce Continuum* chart (see worksheet overleaf). They can act out what it would mean to have consumed that level of hot sauce, which can help express feelings with movement when someone might have difficulty using words. The group leader can then help the expression of these feelings.

Setting the purpose

In order to build a supportive group, it is helpful to observe and give feedback when appropriate. When we give feedback to others, it builds trust and strengthens relationships. This also helps build the skills to ultimately work together in a group, especially in performance of scenes.

The following skills are taught and developed in this activity:

- Listening to peers.

- Building group trust.

- Making connections with other.

- Accepting each other's choices in scenes.

Review the expected and unexpected examples of constructive criticism:

- Some unexpected examples include interrupting in class/group setting, insulting remarks, and giving only negative feedback.

- Some expected examples include respecting others' time by not interrupting them and giving positive feedback after some negative feedback.

To prepare for *Hot Sauce*, participants can brainstorm examples of expected and unexpected group feedback. (Have participants also write out a list for themselves.)

Participants can brainstorm the following examples (keep on the board for visual support):

- Times when others gave negative feedback.

- Times when they gave positive feedback.

- Times they felt it was genuine feedback versus malicious feedback.

- Times they felt supported versus unsupported by the feedback.

Each group member will choose one brief example to share with the rest of the group. They will get one minute to talk about their experiences.

Instructions for *Hot Sauce*

1. Brainstorm with the group and write examples of expected/unexpected behaviors.

2. Present the *Hot Sauce Continuum*: Discuss how things start to get hot and build up in the mind and body. Show the group what it might look like and feel like if you had hot sauce burning in your mouth. Show how a light dose of hot sauce might look versus a medium spice sauce versus the intense ghost pepper sauce.

HOT SAUCE CONTINUUM

Participants can utilize the Hot Sauce Continuum to demonstrate when they feel uncomfortable over unexpected behavior, activities they are participating in, or a topic that is causing a feelings reaction. Utilizing the Hot Sauce Continuum can help a participant communicate feelings without having to use words.

Small level of discomfort

Feelings words: irritated, annoyed, uncomfortable

Demonstrate feeling of discomfort by sitting down and fanning your mouth with your hand.

Medium level of discomfort

Feelings words: frustrated, sad

Demonstrate feeling of discomfort by alternating standing up and sitting down and fanning your mouth with your hand.

HUGE level of discomfort

Feelings words: angry, devastated

Demonstrate feeling of discomfort by jumping around, fanning your mouth with your hand rapidly.

Or, if HUGE feelings of sadness, cowering in a corner in the fetal position, rocking while fanning your mouth with your hand.

3. Have the group demonstrate reactions together, while moving up the levels of hot sauce.

4. Help the group members connect to the physical reaction of eating hot sauce by demonstrating unexpected behaviors. The leader will have the participants demonstrate their level of discomfort with the level of hot sauce they have consumed.

5. When the group is ready, begin to create two-person scenes. Each pair can utilize a scene from the given examples above *or* from the list brainstormed by the group *or* they come up with their own.

6. It is recommended that the leader review the appropriateness of the unexpected behaviors chosen before performance. The leader will also help the pairs plan how they will recover the scene or change it into a successful and expected ending.

7. They will first perform the scene with expected behavior(s).

8. Next, they will perform a second time and add the unexpected behavior(s) to the scene.

9. As scenes play out, the audience will be encouraged to demonstrate reactions from the *Hot Sauce Continuum*. The leader can help prompt the audience participants to react accordingly. For example, when unexpected behavior is being demonstrated, a leader can say: "It's getting hot in here...", instead of saying "that's not expected behavior." When the audience members hear the cue, all participants can react accordingly with their *Hot Sauce* expressions.

10. When the exercise is complete, process with the pairs first, then the group as a whole. Discuss how the experience was for them and what parts were comfortable and uncomfortable. Repeat the above steps until all participants have had the chance to perform.

Make sure to review and practice the following:

-   Discomfort—what does it look like?

-   Levels of comfortable and uncomfortable.

-   Facial expressions of the continuum.

-   Notice what makes others uncomfortable and the facial expressions that go with them.

Variation: Pairs can mix it up, where one partner is presenting as expected and the other is presenting as the unexpected.

Wrap up (group discussion)

-   How was the experience for the participants/players?

- How was the experience for the audience members?

- What were the unexpected behaviors?

- How were the unexpected behaviors adjusted into the expected behaviors?

- How did the unexpected scene parts make people feel?

- What did it feel like for the scene participants when they heard the audience members say "Hot Sauce"?

Discussing as a whole group, process what they thought about the experience in general. Point out the general views of how unexpected behaviors make things difficult or uncomfortable.

ATTENTION MONSTER

Sharing group attention (Who's in the spotlight?)

Goals

- To learn, observe, and experience giving and receiving attention. Expand on unexpected ways to get and take attention away from others.

- To encourage the practice of positive social behaviors, while also managing the unexpected ones.

Materials needed

- List of attention-seeking or distracting behaviors in a group setting, to provide as examples for the group as needed:

  - Yelling, laughing at, or challenging peers.

  - Making comments out of turn.

  - Waving hands around to be picked on.

  - Whispering or talking to peers in the group, while the person(s) in action is talking or engaged in a scene.

  - Making fun of group members.

Setting the purpose

To strengthen a supportive group, it is helpful to give and receive attention, while also handling distractions. When we give the group leader our full attention, it builds trust and allows for a fulfilling group experience. This also helps build the skills of working together in a group, to problem solve and help manage distracting peers.

The following skills are taught and developed in this activity:

- Observing peers.

- Listening to peers.

- Building group trust.

- Dealing with distractions.

To prepare for *Attention Monster*, participants can brainstorm examples of ways to distract the group. (Have participants also write out a list for themselves.) Participants can brainstorm the following examples (keep on the board for visual support):

- Times when others distracted the group.

- Times when they distracted a group.

- Times they felt uncomfortable with the distraction.

- Times they felt the need to intervene in managing the distraction.

Each group member will choose one brief example to share with the rest of the group.

Instructions for *Attention Monster*

1. Brainstorm with the group and write examples of ways to be distracting in a group setting.

2. Define and review what the Attention Monster is. (Example: person who distracts the group.)

3. The leader will choose one participant to become the Attention Monster. (Everyone should get a turn to be the Attention Monster, so this process may take a few sessions to complete.)

4. Have participants sit/stand in a circle.

5. Take the chosen Attention Monster aside and help them choose just one behavior for them to perform.

   - Or review and plan on what that behavior will be ahead of time.

   - This can also be done by the leader randomly assigning a behavior to the Attention Monster or offering a list of behaviors for them to choose from.

6. The leader will start up a random group discussion or activity. (Example Improv game: *Zip-Zap-Zop* or a discussion about "favorite things.")

7. The leader will prompt the Attention Monster to act out with attention-seeking behavior(s).

8. Behavior(s) should be distracting enough to annoy the group or ruin the activity for them.

9. The leader will stop the Attention Monster when all the participants seem to have reached their peak of distraction.

Variation: Instead of participants sitting in a circle, pair the participants off or create groups of three. For pairs: one is the Attention Monster and the other is the focused participant. For the group of three: two participants focus on the task and the third participant is the Attention Monster. This variation can help if the group size is larger or if some group members are uncomfortable with performing in front of the whole group.

Optional: Drama/Play

The group can put on a play, with a plan of having an Attention Monster ruin the play experience. The play can be based on a random topic or a reenactment of a common fable that is short and well known (example: Humpty Dumpty falling off the wall). Throughout the play experience, the Attention Monster will come in during the short scenes and ruin it! Process the discomfort and experiences, on both sides, with the group as a whole.

Wrap up (group discussion)

- What was the Attention Monster doing to distract people?

- How did the Attention Monster make it difficult for everyone?

- In what ways was it uncomfortable being the Attention Monster?

- How did it feel for the group?

Discussing as a whole group, process what they thought about the experience in general. Point out the general views of how being an Attention Monster can make things difficult or uncomfortable.

SPOTLIGHT

Sharing and supporting group attention

Goals

- To learn, observe, and experience giving and sharing group attention.

- Expand on unexpected ways to work together in a performance, while also highlighting your peers.

- Encouraging the practice of reading social cues and following eye gaze as well.

Materials needed

- Flashlight, wand, stick, pointer, etc.

Setting the purpose

To strengthen a supportive group, it is helpful to support peers and work together. When we give the group leader our full attention, it builds trust and allows for a fulfilling group experience. This also helps build the skill of discovering the talents of our fellow peers, while working together in a group performance. Some examples are:

- Listening to peers.

- Observing peers.

- Building group trust.

- Highlighting others instead of ourselves.

To prepare for *Spotlight*, participants can brainstorm examples of ways to support group members in a performance. (Have participants also write out a list for themselves.)

Participants can brainstorm the following examples (keep on the board for visual support):

- Times when others helped the group.

- Times when they felt supported by the group.

- Times they felt uncomfortable or ignored by the group.

- Times they highlighted fellow peers' talents.

Each group member will choose one brief example to share with the rest of the group. They will get a minute to talk about their experiences.

Instructions for *Spotlight*

1. Have the participants performing line up next to each other, in the stage area.

2. Choose one participant to be the director's Spotlight. (The Leader can serve as the Spotlight for the first run, to show how the game works.)

3. The Spotlight will hold a prop (Example: a wand, stick, flashlight, or pointer of some kind), which they will randomly point at other participants in the group.

4. Take turns, allowing for all participants to have an experience as the Spotlight and as a performer being singled out by the Spotlight.

5. The participant that is being pointed to will then begin any random action that they choose. This action will represent themselves in that moment. (Example: moving their bodies, dancing, making a noise, singing.)

6. The Spotlight acts like a conductor, in that they are directing the person who is chosen to act out and showcase themselves in that moment. Once the participant playing the Spotlight moves the spotlight, the participant in action immediately stops and allows the next chosen participant to begin their chosen action.

7. Once all participants get a chance to act out individually and have established their "sound" or "action," they will then wait for the conductor to direct everyone to act out their movements at once, in one giant Spotlight moment. This will be symbolized with the Spotlight simply holding out both of their hands and giving the cue for all to join at once.

8. After all participants react as a group, they will be asked to join together in somehow combining their actions and complimenting each other. For example, if one person has a motion that shows cranking a handle, another participant would wait for the person to crank the handle which would produce their movement in response.

9. Once joint actions are created, the leader will then ask the group to freeze into "stage picture." They will stay in that position for a minute and look around/observe each other supporting the group as a whole.

Optional: Take a temporary digital picture to let the group see how they look. Process the picture and allow time for the group to enjoy the moments of creating something together. (Note: Obtain necessary release for the use of pictures.)

To add a challenge:

• Eliminate the prop and use hand motions only.

• Use eye contact only.

Variation: To modify this exercise for participants that work best in smaller groups, triads can be formed. This calls for one Spotlight/conductor and two performers. This also allows for a more controlled and private performance.

Wrap up (group discussion)
Discuss the experience of how it felt:

• to be an individual, in the group

• to collaborate with others, in the group

• to collaborate together, as a whole group

• at the end of the performance and the resulting group stage picture

• for the Spotlight, being the conductor.

Discussing as a whole group, process what they thought about the experience in general. Point out the general views of how taking the Spotlight makes things difficult or uncomfortable.

SUMMARY

When working with groups, establishing structure, expectations, and boundaries is of great importance. Chapter 2 focused on the structure of the groups, general rules and expectations as applied to Social Theatre™ groups, and how to establish boundaries. Activities ranged from learning how to participate in a group, to sharing the attention in a performance group setting. In Chapter 3, we want to help strengthen group connections, which is why the importance of eye contact and deepening social relationships will be explored.

STRENGTHENING EYE CONTACT AND DEEPENING SOCIAL RELATIONSHIPS

Many of our young people have difficulty with eye contact. Whether this is because of self-confidence, difficulty with social skills, or because of a diagnosis such as anxiety or Autism; practicing eye contact through the following games in this chapter can be helpful. Research has demonstrated that eye contact engages parts of the brain that are needed for socialization and for empathy (Koike *et al.*, 2019). Through practice, eye contact can increase and feel more comfortable, which can lead to better social skills. In this chapter, there are fun activities to help increase and encourage eye contact.

CIRCLE NAME GAME (WITH LEVELED CHALLENGES)

Building connections through eye contact

Goals

- To learn, observe, and experience joint attention.

- Expand on simple "ice-breaker" games so participants are encouraged to make eye contact. Encouraging the practice of reading social cues and following eye gaze as well.

Setting the purpose

This game can be utilized as a get-to-know-you game, as participants will utilize names when passing the ball. Participants are to make eye contact when passing the ball and saying a person's name.

Special note: For peers on the Autism spectrum who feel especially uncomfortable with eye contact, work within their limits and apply no pressure to use eye contact consistently throughout this activity.

Instructions for *Circle Name Game*

1. The group stands in a circle.

2. Person A says the name of Person B across the circle, passing them the ball.

3. Person B says the name of Person C, passing Person C the ball.

4. Continue several times.

Challenges

- *Challenge A:* Pass ball with noise and eye contact only. Allow group members to copy person before or make their own noise.

- *Challenge B:* Pass imaginary dart with noise and eye contact.

- *Challenge C:* Pass imaginary dart with eye contact only.

Wrap up (group discussion)

- What skill was this game practicing?

- How do you feel making eye contact with others?

- How did you feel when others made eye contact with you?

- Why is eye contact important?

Discussing as a whole group, process what they thought about the experience in general.

CONNECTING WITH EYE CONTACT

Note: This activity is an adaptation of the *"Cross Circle"* Improv game.[1]

Goals

- To learn, observe, and experience joint attention.

- Expand on reading social cues, paying attention to social cues, and increasing joint eye gaze.

Setting the purpose

The group is working on eye contact to communicate with others. Participants must stand in a circle and communicate with eye contact, pointing, and saying "Yes."

Special note: For peers on the Autism spectrum who feel especially uncomfortable with

---

1   See http://improvencyclopedia.org/games/Cross_Circle.html

eye contact, work within their limits and apply no pressure to use eye contact consistently throughout this activity.

Instructions

1. The group stands in a circle. Person A points to Person B across the circle.

2. Person B says "Yes" giving permission for Person A to take Person B's spot.

3. Before Person B moves from his/her spot, Person B points to Person C.

4. Person C responds with "Yes" to give permission for Person B to take his/her spot.

5. Continue with Person D, E, and so on…

Challenges

- *Challenge A:* Take away "Yes" and only use pointing and nodding.

- *Challenge B:* Take away pointing and only use nodding.

Wrap up (group discussion)

- What skills do you think we were working on?

- What social cues did you have to pay attention to?

- What was fun about this game?

- What was challenging?

Discussing as a whole group, process what they thought about the experience in general.

JOINT ATTENTION CIRCLE

Strengthening eye contact

Goals

- To practice and experience joint attention.

- Expand on reading social cues, increasing awareness of others, and eye gaze.

- Decrease performance anxiety over making mistakes.

Setting the purpose

In Butterworth and Jarrett's (1991) study, the development of joint attention was found to occur by an average of 18 months. This means a typically developing 18-month-old is able to follow another person's eye gaze to where they are looking. However, some who struggle with social cognitive deficits may still have difficulty with joint attention. Gernsbacher and colleagues (2008) found that joint attention in children can look different from in adults, as they might point to initiate joint attention.

In the Social Thinking® Methodology, it is referred to as "Thinking with your eyes," as discussed in *Thinking About You, Thinking About Me* (Garcia Winner, 2007) and used within several of their curricula and storybooks.

Before introducing the game, teach the participants about the concept of "joint attention" and why it is important. An example of what you might say is: "Does anyone know what joint attention is? Joint attention is when I look over here, you will also look to see where I am looking. Let's practice. I'm looking somewhere, who can tell me where I am looking? Why is it important to know where someone is looking? That's right. It is important so we can know what someone might like, not like, or be thinking about."

Thus, the following activity can be utilized to increase joint attention, by noticing the social cue of head movement. The key to this game is being able to increase the speed without messing up. When someone messes up, have all participants cheer about the mess up to lessen the anxiety about the mistake. Then restart the game.

Special note: For peers on the Autism spectrum who feel especially uncomfortable with eye contact, work within their limits and apply no pressure to use eye contact consistently throughout this activity.

Instructions for *Joint Attention Circle*

1. Practice turn of head to the person on the right with eye contact, person on the right uses eye contact and turn of head to pass eye contact to the next person on the right, the group continue to pass eye contact to the right around the circle.

2. Once this is understood and smooth, add the challenge of reversing the eye contact in the circle. Thus, one person will decide not to look at the next person on the right, but instead look back at the person to their left. The person to their left now needs to make eye contact and pass it around the circle to the left. Group members can reverse directions at any time.

3. Increase speed. Remember to cheer any mistakes.

Wrap up (group discussion)

- What skills were we working on?

- Why was joint eye gaze important in this game?

- What would have happened if joint eye gaze wasn't used?

- What was easy for you? What was hard?

- What made it fun?

Discussing as a whole group, process what they thought about the experience in general.

JOINT ATTENTION CIRCLE WORKSHEET

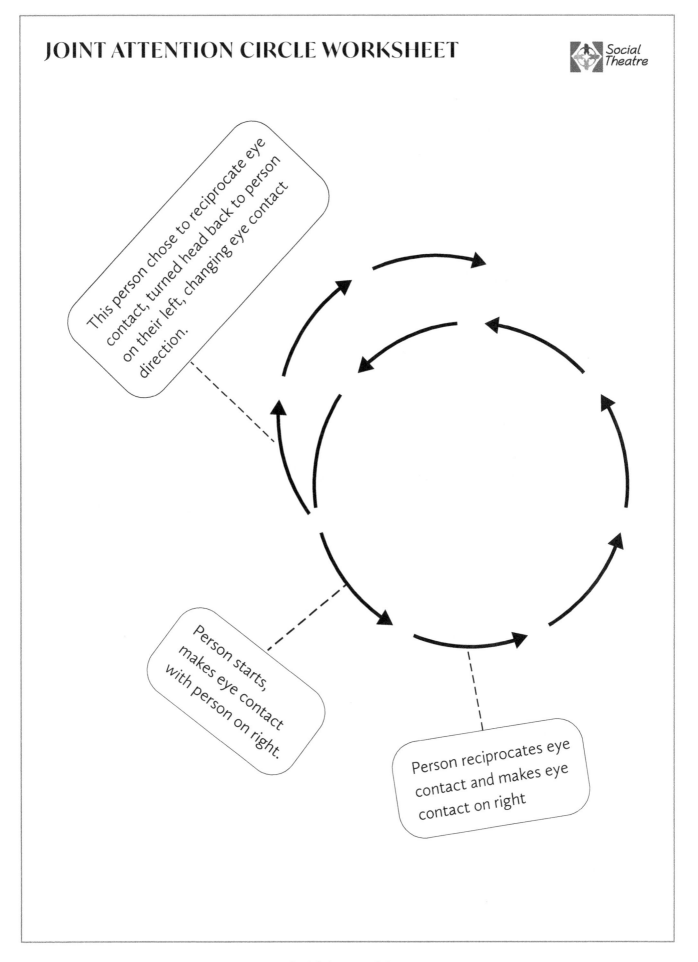

This person chose to reciprocate eye contact, turned head back to person on their left, changing eye contact direction.

Person starts, makes eye contact with person on right.

Person reciprocates eye contact and makes eye contact on right

PASSING THE BALL

Practicing joint attention

Goals

- To practice group-based joint attention and eye gaze.

- Expand on increasing awareness of social cues and group members.

Materials needed

- A ball.

Setting the purpose

Like the previous activity, the *Joint Attention Circle*, this one also focuses on joint attention. In this game, we will be utilizing our eyes to look at who others are looking at, which we have to keep track of so we are aware when it might be our turn.

Special note: For peers on the Autism spectrum who feel especially uncomfortable with eye contact, work within their limits and apply no pressure to use eye contact consistently throughout this activity.

Instructions for *Passing the Ball*

1. For the first couple of rounds, utilize a ball.

2. Person A demonstrates first by looking directly in Person B's eyes, says Person B's name and then throws the ball. Person B catches the ball.

3. Person B chooses a Person C. Person B says Person C's name and passes the ball, and so on.

4. After one or two rounds, take away the ball. Person A look into Person B's eyes and says Person B's name, Person A pretends to pass the ball. Person B pretends to catch the ball.

Challenge

Take away the movement of passing and catching the ball. Person A chooses a Person B and states Person B's name with eye contact. Person B chooses a Person C and says Person's C's name with eye contact, and so on. Utilize the ball for the first couple of rounds. The leader demonstrates first by looking directly in someone's eyes and says someone else's name with eye contact. Then take away the ball, look in someone's eyes and say other's names with an imaginary ball.

Variation

This game can also be utilized as a getting-to-know-you game to practice names.

Wrap up (group discussion)

- What skills were we working on?

- Why was joint eye gaze important in this game?

- What would have happened if joint eye gaze wasn't used?

- What was easy for you? What was hard?

- What made it fun?

Discussing as a whole group, process what they thought about the experience in general.

MIRRORING THE MIRROR

Strengthening joint attention

Goals

- To practice and experience group-based joint attention.

- Expand on reading social cues and awareness of group members.

Setting the purpose

Review the concept of eye contact, following another's eye gaze, and joint attention. In teaching eye gaze, group members have to look at the group leader's eye gaze in order to notice where the leader is looking. They are also looking at and noticing the movements of the group leader and movements of those in the room with them.

Special note: For peers on the Autism spectrum who feel especially uncomfortable with eye contact, work within their limits and apply no pressure to use eye contact consistently throughout this activity.

Instructions for *Mirroring the Mirror*

1. Participant A stands in front of the room. Other group members stay in their seats.

2. Participant A will look around and choose one other person (Participant B) to mirror.

3. Participant A will copy everything Participant B does.

4. Once the other participants figure out who Participant A is mirroring, they will also copy Participant B.

5. The last person who mirrors Participant B is chosen to go in front of the room and become Participant A.

6. The new Participant A starts the game over by repeating steps 1–5.

Wrap up (group discussion)

- How did this experience feel to you?

- What did you feel when you were being mirrored?

- How did you feel when you were mirroring someone else?

- What was more challenging for you, being mirrored or mirroring someone else? What made that difficult?

- What felt more comfortable to you? And how did others contribute to making you comfortable?

Discussing as a whole group, process what they thought about the experience in general.

SUMMARY

After establishing the structure and flow of the groups in Chapter 2, Chapter 3 focused on strengthening group connections. A first step to recognizing social cues is to utilize eye contact, notice others' eye gaze direction, what they are doing, and their possible wants. By applying activities based on strengthening eye contact and deepening social relationships, better social skills will likely be the result. In Chapter 4 we move on to reading social cues, which not only deepens social interactions but strengthens relationships overall.

READING SOCIAL CUES

To read social situations and understand perspectives, one must be able to understand facial expressions, note what is happening in the environment, sustain joint attention, and notice what people are doing. Essentially, the first step in reading social cues is understanding joint attention. Specifically, the idea of being able to think about others and what they think about you (Garcia Winner, 2007). The following activities presented are for practicing and gaining a better understanding of joint attention.

WHAT CHANGES

Discovering details

Goals

- To practice and experience the process of noticing and remembering detail in the environment.

- To utilize eyes and thought processes to remember details in the environment.

- To use self-control to not give clues which will give away answers.

Setting the purpose

This activity practices social cue recognition and executive functioning of working verbal/non-verbal memory as participants have to guess what has changed. For populations with more social cue recognition difficulty, changes need to be more obvious. Those who have more nuanced social difficulty should try to find subtle changes. The group will also be working on how to maintain a "poker face" so they do not give away the answer on what was changed. Then, if needed, they will work on slowly giving small hints until the answer is found.

Instructions for *What Changes*

1. Have a couple of people leave the room.

2. The other participants in the room will change something about the room.

3. Those who left the room will come back in and look around trying to figure out what was changed.

Variation

Have someone leave the room and change something about him/herself. Have the person come back in the room and have the others guess what he/she changed.

Challenge

Have a group stand outside, and have a person change something about him/herself in the environment or something in the room. For example, the participant can change how or where they are sitting or change something in the room. Then, have the others come in and try to figure out what a person in the room changed about him/herself.

Wrap up (group discussion)

- What did you feel about this activity? Was it easy? Hard?

- What was easy/hard about it?

- What skill or senses were you using to figure this out?

- Think of some situations where you will need the skill of remembering non-verbal/verbal details and recognizing changed social cues.

Discussing as a whole group, process what they thought about the experience in general.

DO YOU WANT TO SEE THIS?

Recognizing others' wants

Goals

- To practice and experience the process of recognizing what other people need.

- Expand on joint attention.

Materials needed

- Random objects—some that interest the participants, some that might disgust them or may be boring to participants.

- Arrow worksheet.

Setting the purpose and teaching concepts

The leader will inquire with participants to check understanding of joint attention, which Michelle Garcia Winner, creator of the Social Thinking® Methodology, refers to in her concept of "Thinking with your eyes" (Garcia Winner, 2007). The leader can look at something and ask participants to identify what she/he is looking at and thinking about. When the participants answer, they will discuss how they knew that the leader was thinking about the object they were looking at. Then, the leader will use the arrow to discuss whether they tracked the eye gaze of the leader to find their answer.

Instructions for *Do You Want to See This?*

1. Leader will place objects all over the room.

2. First, model the activity to the participants. Use your eye gaze to stare at something you are thinking about. Another person will guess what you are thinking about.

3. Have a participant repeat step one, this person will be Participant A.

4. The leader will model this next step by looking at Participant A's eyes in a big dramatic fashion, following the eye gaze to the object. If needed, the leader will use an arrow to follow the eye gaze of the participant to the object.

5. The leader (Participant B) will take the object that Participant A is looking at and ask, "Do you want to see this?"

6. Choose a Participant B to model the leader's behavior. Participant A will look at something, Participant B will pick up the item and say, "Do you want to see this?" (Please see the scripted speech bubble on the next page.)

Challenges

Note: All of the challenges below involve making a feeling-based face (e.g., disgust, fear, disinterest, or happiness). How the challenge evolves will depend on which expression is being used.

*   *Challenge A:* Look at that object and make a simple feeling-based face. Participant B will identify whether or not she/he wants the object.

*   *Challenge B:* Discuss why a person might be looking at the object with that feeling expression. Participant B will decide, does Participant A want the object? Why might they feel this way about the object?

*   *Challenge C:* What might be a comment you could say to someone who is looking at the object with that facial expression? Try again with a response. The other participant can respond in return, beginning an Improvised scene.

Do you want to see this?

Wrap up (group discussion)

- What did you feel about this activity?

- Was it easy? What parts were more difficult?

- When might you need to use this skill of recognizing what someone wants?

- Why might you need to recognize how they feel once you offer it?

Discussing as a whole group, begin to process what they thought about the experience in general.

THE HUDDLE

Group problem solving

Goals

- To practice slowing down and processing problems.

- To better utilize our senses to practice problem solving in a group setting.

Materials needed

- *The Huddle* worksheet (see at the end of this section).

Activity set-up and teaching concepts

This activity demonstrates the importance of listening to each other, collaboration, and teamwork. To teach problem solving, the "Look, Think, Idea" process can be practiced, in order to utilize it eventually during real-time collaborative problem solving. The strategy slows down and dramatizes problem solving, making the process more fun and memorable. The group goes through *The Huddle*'s "Look, Think, and Idea" steps together. These should be practiced in set-up problem scenarios or in plays, and when ready it can be utilized in real-time simple problem solving.

Gathering social clues through utilizing our senses is important to figure out problems and situations. In 1978, Premack and Woodruff studied chimpanzees and discovered that the chimpanzees were able to understand a deeper perspective of others' desires, wants, and needs, namely "Theory of Mind." From information we gather from the social environment, participants can make a guess about what might be happening or someone's perspective. Michelle Garcia Winner and Pamela Crooke help build these social competencies in young learners in their book *You Are a Social Detective* (2020). Moreover, the book teaches how to look for social "clues" in a situation such as noticing where you are (place), who is present, and what is happening.

Warm up

Demonstrate the concepts of Look, Think, and Idea separately.

Look

Have participants line up. Teach passing the eye contact with the word "Look" while pointing at an object, telling the next person to look. The next person points at the object and says "Look"; the next person looks then looks at the next person saying "Look" until everyone has pointed, looked, and said look. The goal is to pass the action of looking around the group, and to speed up the process.

To increase the challenge and to be able to utilize this in real-time problem solving, participants can try the "Look" around the circle, without pointing, only with the use of eye contact. In a social situation, pointing might be misinterpreted. However, it is a good place to start with those who might struggle with joint eye contact. The arrow worksheet can also be utilized from the last lesson.

Think

Demonstrate what thinking looks like.

Say, "It can take longer to think how to solve a problem than to feel feelings. Let's demonstrate thinking for a bit longer."

Idea

Demonstrate what it looks like when you get an idea. What does your face look like? What does your body look like? Make it bigger. Say "Idea!" and put your finger in the air.

Instructions for *The Huddle*

1. The first step is to brainstorm a simple problem. Here are a few examples:

   - Pencil is broken.

   - Water on the floor.

   - Dropped books/papers.

   - Spelled a word wrong.

   - No chair at the desk I need to sit at.

   - No space for me at the table.

2. Next, choose a problem scenario and set it up. Participants can participate by following the steps of problem solving through using *The Huddle* with the "Look, Think, Idea" steps as follows.

The Huddle's "Look, Think, Idea" strategy has three different parts. The steps are as follows:

The leader can look at the participants and with exaggerated body, voice, and facial expression, point at the problem and say (over time, take away the point and just use eyes to look back and forth):

"We are looking: Look! (Use your eyes to notice.)

What is the problem? What are people doing? What are people feeling?"

The next step is "Think." The leader will demonstrate by exaggerating a confused facial expression by scratching their chin, tapping their lip, scratching their head, and saying, "Hmm..." Participants will demonstrate along with the teacher, "Hmmm...."
Pull everyone into a huddle and say:

"Hmm... We are thinking: Think! (Scratching chins and heads.)

What should I/we do? What is the plan?"

- Participants can respond with answers.

- If possible, write ideas on the board and use them as a visual.

- The group decides what solution they are going to implement, who will help and how they will implement the solution.

  - If many solutions are given, it is okay to repeat Look, Think, Idea until each participant's problem solving idea is practiced.

After the group decides on what solution they are going to implement, they can move to the next step.

Put a finger in the air and yell, *"Idea!"*

Have those who were going to demonstrate how to fix the problem show how. The next time *The Huddle* is used, it can be utilized with faster speed, with all participants following the motions of Look, Think, Idea together. When the group has role played it enough, it can be utilized in a play or in a real-time problem scenario.

Cool down after activity is completed
In a circle, the group can cool down by synchronously doing Look, Think, Idea movements.

Wrap up (group discussion)

- Why is it important to use Look, Think, Idea?

- What does this help with? (Taking our time helps us to think more clearly, which helps us come up with ways to fix situations.)

- Why should we take our time when trying to solve a problem?

Discussing as a whole group, process what they thought about the experience in general.

THE HUDDLE

Look!

What is the problem? What are people doing? What are people feeling?

Think!

What should I/we do? What is the plan?

Idea!

Demonstrate how to fix the problem.

WHERE DID THAT COME FROM?

Building listening skills

Goals

- To practice and experience the process of using ears and closely listening to voices.

- Expand on determining the direction of voices and the people that are doing the communicating.

- Think about others' voices and perspectives; predict what they might say.

Setting the purpose

This activity can be utilized for any topic or brainstorm, from a list of science terms to a list of greeting phrases. This activity calls upon participants to utilize what they know about others, such as the sound of their voices and their favored phrases. Participants can also observe who is sitting in different locations and utilize their ears to gauge which direction a voice is coming from, to help identify who might have spoken.

Instructions for *Where Did That Come From?*

1. Brainstorm and write a list of words and phrases that can be used in greeting others.

2. Tell everyone to look at the list to decide what phrase they will share.

3. Have everyone close their eyes or look down.

4. The leader taps someone on their shoulder, and the person tapped will say one of the words or phrases that came from the brainstorm.

Variation

Brainstorm and use different lists, such as personality traits or interests and hobbies.

Wrap up (group discussion)

- What skill were you working on in this game?

- What were clues you recognized when being able to tell who said what?

- When do you need to be able to use your ears in social situations?

Discussing as a whole group, process what they thought about the experience in general.

ROLE PLAY: MUTUAL EYE GAZE AND RECOGNIZING BOREDOM

Our participants might miss the social cue of what it looks like to bore others during a conversation. Some factors might come into play, such as not recognizing what boredom looks like in someone's eyes, facial expression, or body expression. For our clients, students, or participants who might struggle with what to say or how to respond, this role playing activity can help by first breaking down the expression, then the response.

DEALING WITH BOREDOM

Goals

- To practice and experience the process of recognizing social cues, such as boredom.

- Expand on making good observations during social exchanges.

- To recognize drifting attention and when someone can be pulled back into the conversation.

Setting the purpose

Lead a discussion by asking participants to demonstrate what boredom looks like.

- Eyes will be looking away more.

- Body posture may not be square.

- Maybe looking at phone or something else.

What situations might people get bored of?

- Class.

- Lecture or long ceremonial talk.

- Person who is talking too much.

What might happen if people get bored when in a conversation with us?

- If someone is getting bored, they might leave the conversation.

- They might tune us out and not listen.

- They might feel that we are not giving them a chance to talk.

However, we want others to listen to us, and we also want to listen to others. When we listen, it makes others feel good about us.

Demonstrate together levels of boredom using eye contact. Second time through, add body language.

- Interested.

- A bit distracted.

- Bored and disinterested.

- Very bored and disinterested.

Roles

- Person who is listening (eventually gets bored).

- Person who is talking.

For practice in recognizing boredom in others, we will role play and respond.

Instructions for *Dealing with Boredom*

1. Determine the topic of conversation.

2. Leader will choose two participants to role play the conversation.

   Participant 1: Talking and asking questions.

   Participant 2: Listens for a while, then demonstrates not being interested by averting eye gaze.

Freeze! Is the conversation salvageable? Has Participant 2 completely disengaged? (Discuss how you know.) *Unfreeze!*

3. If Participant 2 has not completely disengaged (body begins turning or stepping back), Participant 1 can then ask a question.

4. Participant 1 will recognize Participant 2's drifting eye contact and ask Participant 2 a question. The question should be about a common interest or something Participant 2 likes in order to gain their attention. In gauging whether a person wants to be pulled back into a conversation or whether there is motivation to discuss the topic, they should consider Participant 2's body language and how it demonstrates a level of interest.

5. Allow participants the chance to switch roles or take turns in each role, so everyone has the opportunity to experience the different perspectives.

Wrap up (group discussion)

- What did you feel about this activity?

- In what role did you feel uncomfortable? Why?

- In what role did you feel comfortable? Why?

- When could you use this skill?

Discuss as a whole group, processing what they thought about the experience in general.

SUMMARY

Joint attention is key in reading social situations and understanding perspectives. This chapter utilized activities that sparked the concept of being able to think about others and what they think about you. In Chapter 5, we expand on noticing other social cues, such as the environment and the feelings of others.

RECOGNIZING AND EXPRESSING FEELINGS

To be able to accurately read social situations and understand perspectives, people must also be able to recognize and express feelings. The idea of being able to think about others and what they think about you is key (*Thinking About You, Thinking About Me*, Garcia Winner, 2007). Adding the additional layer of developing empathy, where you are able to feel what others are feeling, can be a tricky concept for some. The following activities presented are for practicing, better recognizing, and expressing feelings—especially when engaged in social situations with peers.

THE CHASE

Recognizing and expressing feelings

Introduction

In the first Social Theatre™ book (Amador, 2018), the play "Stop Chasing Me" demonstrates the concept of emotional reciprocity. In the play, one actor chases another actor. But their feelings don't match because the first actor forgot to ask the other actor to play chase. Therefore, the other actor felt scared.

The chase scene is a powerful tool for being able to recognize emotions in action. The chase scene emotions can be utilized to demonstrate a response to another person's emotional response as well as determine what story might create the emotional dynamic.

Goal

- Practicing expressing and recognizing emotions, as well as being able to read possible scenarios when two emotions are tied to a game of chase.

Setting the purpose

To help our participants to be able to recognize others' emotions, we must teach them how to make smart guesses as in *You Are a Social Detective* (Winner and Crooke, 2020). The strategy involves "thinking with your eyes" to recognize the environment, who is around, and what is happening, and listening to what others are saying and thinking about what they are doing, which can help children figure out social clues and interpret situations so they can know what to do or what might come next.

The chase scene can be used to teach about using our eyes to recognize social cues.

The Chase rules

1. The participants are playing characters. In the chase scene, their characters' jobs are only to reflect one feeling.

2. Each participant's role is only to chase or be chased.

3. The characters pretend to chase but are actually not trying to catch up with each other.

Note: *The Chase*, along with specific feelings, could invoke certain triggers or negative feelings, thus choose feelings carefully and allow participants to choose the feelings and scenes they feel comfortable in.

In a clinical/therapeutic setting

The Chase can be utilized to help rewire negative and traumatic experiences. The feelings given to the chaser and chasee can be based on experiences that need to be brought out and rewired. To distance triggers, the play "Stop Chasing Me" from *Teaching Social Skills through Sketch Comedy and Improv Games* (Amador, 2018) can be taught and, when learning and practicing the chase scene, different feelings can be tried. The background chase music can also help to distance negative or traumatic experiences. Also, the client can be given a choice about the ending and can enact the ending they choose.

In a school/community setting

The Chase can be utilized to help participants put together possible clues to read social situations as well as the opportunity to implement problem-solving strategies. However, it is important to be mindful of your participants and possible triggering scenarios. The following are examples that most likely are not triggering:

- Angry Chaser, Happy Chasee.

- Surprised Chaser, Confused Chasee.

- Happy Chaser, Confused Chasee.

- Scared Chaser, Happy Chasee.

- Happy Chaser, Angry Chasee.

Instructions for *The Chase*

1. The leader should demonstrate the act of chasing, in a slow chase with a participant. In this case, the leader will never catch up with the participant. In order to add

humor, the leader can also go very slowly, while adding exaggerated facial and body expressions (e.g., hands in the air).

2. Have participants take turns with role playing being the chaser or the one being chased. When participants are ready and able to demonstrate self-control, as in not needing to catch up to the one being chased, the leader can turn on the Benny Hill Theme song for chase music and enhancing humor. If certain participants do not feel comfortable taking a specific role, it is okay to change the scene so they feel comfortable, in order to avoid invoking any negative or traumatic memories.

3. The Social Formula is Social Thinking's (Winner and Crooke, 2020) method to recognize social cues by using what we see, what we hear, and what we know to decipher social situations. Once someone notices these social cues and is able to put together the information, they can make a "smart guess" about what is happening.

4. Ask for two participants and quietly assign one feeling for the actor who is chasing and assign another feeling for the actor who is being chased. After reminding the participants that they must follow the same format of not catching up to each other, say "Lights, Camera, Action!", and start the Benny Hill Theme song music for the participants to begin the scene.

5. Once the participants have had enough time to display their scene, have them stretch and shake their bodies in order to shake off the character they were playing. Then they can rejoin the group.

The Chase *scene emotional recognition and reciprocity*

Participant 1: "The Chaser" feeling is . . . .

Participant 2: "Being Chased" feeling is . . . .

Have the other participants choose a feeling for each of them.

Wrap up (group discussion)
Discussing as a whole group, begin by processing what they thought about the experience in general.

- What might be happening in this situation?

- How might both people feel?

- How might others feel who are witnessing?

- What could happen if the situation continued?

- What could they do to resolve the situation?

EYE PASS EMO PASS

Connecting eyes and emotions

Goals

- To learn, observe, and experience giving and sharing eye contact and joint attention.

- Increase understanding of facial expressions and facial emotion recognition skills.

- Encourage the practice of reading facial expressions and labeling emotions.

Setting the purpose

To strengthen relationships, it is helpful to support peers and recognize how they are feeling. When we give peers our full attention, it builds trust and allows for an honest group experience. This also helps build deeper relationships with our fellow peers. Being able to identify basic emotions from people's facial expressions is a key factor in good communication. Some examples of emotions are:

- Sad.

- Bored.

- Happy.

- Scared.

- Anxious.

- Frustrated.

To prepare for *Eye Pass Emo Pass*, participants can brainstorm examples of emotions, as well as ways to support peers that express them. (Have participants also write out a list for themselves.)

Participants can brainstorm the following examples (keep on the board for visual support):

- Times when they ignored or missed a facial expression.

- Times they misread a facial expression.

- Times they didn't give or receive good eye contact.

- Times they felt misunderstood by peers.

- Times they misunderstood a peer.

- Times they were frustrated with social interaction.

- Times they were scared of social interaction.

- Times they were bored by social interaction.

- Times they were sad because of social interaction.

Each group member will choose one brief example to share with the rest of the group. They will get a minute to talk about their experiences.

Instructions for *Eye Pass Emo Pass*

1. Create a circle for the entire group.

2. One person starts off with choosing an emotion, then places that emotion on their face. That person then holds the emotion on their face, while sending their eye contact to a random person in the circle.

3. The person receiving the eye contact and facial expression of emotion has to say the first person's name—acknowledging they received the eye contact correctly.

4. This next person guesses what emotion the group member sent them, along with holding their eye contact.

5. The group member that sent the emotion holds the emotion on their face, until the receiving member guesses correctly. When the emotion is guessed correctly, the sender can release their facial expression.

6. The group member who guessed the emotion then morphs their face in the chosen emotional expression they want.

7. The group member then sends eye contact to another random person in the group and starts the whole game again.

Variation: Pairs

To modify this exercise for participants who work best in smaller groups, pairs can be formed. Essentially, the same game is played with only two people. This allows for a simplified version of the game and a chance to hold eye contact the entire time they are working together. They simply pass the emotional expression back and forth with their partner, while allowing for each to guess what emotion they are expressing. This version allows for more time to be spent connecting and practicing these skills.

Wrap up (group discussion)

Discuss the experience of how it felt:

- to collaborate with others in the group

- to collaborate with a partner (if the pair option was chosen)

- to read emotions on faces

- to express emotions on faces.

VOICE MESSAGE

Tone matching and feelings puppet

Goals

- To learn, observe, and experience voice control, vocal expression, and meaning behind the voice.

- Expand on increasing the reading of emotions behind vocal expressions.

- Encouraging the practice of non-verbal and verbal communication skills.

Setting the purpose

To strengthen communication, it is helpful to be able to read the emotions behind people's tone of voice. This also helps build deeper connections with our fellow peers. Being able to identify basic emotions from people's voice tone helps support good communication. Some examples of emotions are:

- Sad.

- Bored.

- Happy.

- Scared.

- Anxious.

- Frustrated.

To prepare for *Voice Message,* participants can brainstorm examples of voice tones with their matching emotions. They can also talk about ways to support peers that express them. You can expand by discussing scenarios where certain voice tones are expected versus not.

   Participants can brainstorm the following examples (keep on the board for visual support):

- Times when they misread/or missed a voice tone expression.

- Times they didn't express the correct voice tone.

- Times they felt misunderstood by peers.

Each group member will choose one brief example to share with the rest of the group. They will get a minute to talk about their experiences.

Warm up and practice

1. Brainstorm and write down participant ideas about different types of voices, tones in voices, and what those tones mean.

2. Group similar ideas, then write at least one example phrase for each type of voice.

3. Role play the voice tones and expressions for the group. Demonstrate how it sounds when expressing certain voice tones from the list the group created.

4. Allow the group to practice a few voice tones in unison. Use this as a warm-up for the group, as well as for their voices.

Instructions for *Voice Message*

1. After the warm-up is complete, choose one person to start off the game.

2. They will then choose an emotion, place it in their voice, and alter their voice tone and match the emotion with a phrase (e.g., "You're in big trouble, mister" would be sent with an angry tone, a stern voice, and a serious looking facial expression).

3. The person in action then holds the emotion in their voice, produces it again while sending it to another random person in the circle. (Performing it twice allows for the group to grasp the tone better and process their guess for longer.)

4. The person receiving the voice, emotion, and eye contact, has to say the person's name—acknowledging they received the voice message.

5. The person receiving the voice message now has to guess what emotion was communicated through the voice tone from the sender, while maintaining eye contact.

6. When the guess is correct, the person who had sent the emotion can release the focus on the receiver. The receiver then becomes the sender. The cycle then repeats with the sender portraying an emotion through voice tone to a receiver, thus repeating the game sequence.

Variation: Pairs

1. The same game above is played with only two people. This allows for a simplified version of holding the tone of voice the entire time they are working together.

2. They pass the tone and emotional expression back and forth with their partner, while allowing for each to guess what emotion they are expressing. This version allows for more time to be spent connecting 1:1 and practicing these skills in a more intimate setting.

Challenge

Have one person stand directly in front of another participant. The person behind is demonstrating a voice tone they choose, while saying dialogue. The person in front is trying to match facial expressions and body movements to the voice tone coming from behind them. Have the other participants guess if the feeling matches the voice tone.

Check in with both the voice tone and the feelings puppet to see if their portrayal of the feelings matched. If not, what could happen in this scenario? Feel free to role play it out.

Wrap up (group discussion)

Discuss the experience of how it felt:

- in general, for you?

- to express your voice?

- to work with the group/your partner?

- *and*: What was easy? What was hard?

Discussing as a whole group, process what they thought about the experience in general.

Note: The following activities are broken up into four versions. Since the theme is the same, exploring feelings and empathy, and they build on each other, we decided it would be easier to simplify the written portion of the activity application to avoid duplication.

MATCHING FEELINGS AND EMPATHY (VERSIONS A, B, C, AND D)

Goals

- Identifying emotions by coordinating facial/body expressions and vocal tone.

- Matching emotions with facial/body expression and vocal tone.

- Exploring empathy and matching it to feelings.

Setting the purpose

Review different types of emotions, feelings, and facial expressions. Discuss what empathy means, how we typically express it, and how it strengthens relationships. You could use visual examples and/or online images and videos to help with this.

Brainstorm with the group and come up with a list for reading others' feelings. Consider:

- What does this specific feeling look like?

- What does their facial expression look like?

- What might their tone sound like?

- What might their words be?

- What are people doing when they are expressing this feeling?

This table shows some common emotions and the ways people express them to get you started.

Reading others' feelings

Feeling of sender	What sender might be doing	What sender's facial expression might look like	Possible tone of sender	Possible words of sender
Anger	Pacing Balled up fist Taking up more space	Eyebrows together Red face Scrunched mouth Darting eyes	Loud Strong	"I can't believe this!" "Ugh! Argh!"
Sadness	Slow movements Shoulders down	Looking down Corners of mouth turned a little down	Soft Gentle	Slow words "I'm so sad" "This is so hard" "This stinks"
Happiness	Calm and smooth movements	Smile Wide eyes Focused eyes/face	Strong Clear	Fast words "This is great!" "Cool" "It's all good" "I'm good, thanks"

VERSION A: *READING OTHERS' EMOTIONS*
Goals

- Exploring emotions, facial expressions, and feelings.

Instructions for *Reading Others' Emotions*

Pair off the group; each pair will do the following:

1. Assign one person (Sender) to express emotions and facial expressions.

2. Assign the other partner to observe (Receiver).

3. The Sender will express an emotion, one at a time.

4. The Receiver will mirror and then identify each of the emotions as they are expressed.

5. Switch roles and repeat.

Wrap up (group discussion)

- What was it like to express feelings and read others' feelings?

- Were you able to guess correctly/express enough?

- What was easier for you? Harder?

- Why is it important to read others' feelings?

- Why is it important to express feelings enough?

Discussing as a whole group, process what they thought about the experience in general.

VERSION B: *READING OTHERS' VOCAL TONES AND BODY/FACIAL EXPRESSIONS*
Goal

- Exploring emotions through reading body expressions and vocal tone.

Materials needed

- Scarves, sunglasses, and masks.

Instructions for *Reading Others' Vocal Tones and Body/Facial Expressions*

1. The sender is the person expressing emotions. He/she will cover his/her face with a scarf or silly glasses with attached nose and mustache.

2. The sender will then express the emotion and facial expression behind the face covering.

3. The observer will listen to the person's vocal tone and watch the body expression, trying to figure out what the sender is trying to express. They then make a guess.

4. The person expressing emotions will then remove the face covering and redo the same expression, allowing the observer to get a clear look of what they were expressing.

5. Switch roles and repeat.

Wrap up (group discussion)

- What was it like to try to read others without the facial expression?

- Were you able to guess correctly or express correctly?

- Was it easier or more difficult? Why?

- Did the tone of voice match the feeling?

- Why is it important for the tone of voice to match the feeling?

Discussing as a whole group, process what they thought about the experience in general.

VERSION C: *MATCHING EMPATHY TO FEELINGS*
Goal

- Reading emotions in order to distinguish what type of empathy to give.

Instructions for *Matching Empathy to Feelings*

1. Start by leading a discussion about what empathy is.

2. Explore how empathy deepens relationships and emotional connections with people.

3. Ask participants to define how and when others have shown them empathy.

4. Brainstorm with the group and create a list of expressing empathy through different emotions.

5. Further explore:

    a. What might that look like?

    b. What are people doing when they are expressing empathy?

    c. What does their face look like?

    d. What might their tone sound like?

    e. What might their words be?

6. Create a chart or add to the example below.

Expressing empathy chart

Feeling of sender	What receiver might be doing	Facial expression of receiver	Tone of receiver	Words of receiver
Anger	Giving space/listening	Calm and concerned	Confident Strong Clear	"That sounds hard." Less talking
Sadness	Getting a little closer, bending down to meet eye contact	A little worried, to show concern	Soft Gentle Light	"I'm so sorry that happened." "How are you coping?"
Happiness	Possible high five, Walking with confidence	Smile, intensity to match other's smile Wide eyes	Strong Clear Loud	"Wow!" "I'm SO happy for you!" "That's so COOL!"

Repeat steps, with an observer and a feelings expresser in each pair.

7. The participant who expresses feelings will choose and express a feeling.

8. The observer will then practice how to respond with facial expression and body movements only.

9. Leader will then guide the observer to add words to match the empathic body movements and facial expressions.

Wrap up (group discussion)

- What did you feel when you were expressing feelings/showing empathy?

- Was it easy/hard to show empathy? Accept empathy?

- Why is it important to show empathy?

- How did you feel when the observer demonstrated empathy?

- Who in your life do you feel empathy from?

Discussing as a whole group, process what they thought about the experience in general.

Expand

Explore "mismatched" facial expressions and emotions. This is when people express one emotion through their actions but display another on their face. (Example: Someone receives a gift they didn't want; they are smiling but not saying "thank you" in a nice way.) For this activity, have one person express an emotion that does not match the facial expression. Have the observer guess what emotion and expression the other is showing. Allow for discussion of how it feels to express mismatched emotions, as well as the experience of observing them.

Wrap up (group discussion)

Discuss the experience of:

- expressing feelings

- working with a partner

- expressing empathy.

Discussing as a whole group, process what they thought about the experience in general.

VERSION D: *MATCHING EMPATHY TO FEELINGS—EXPLORING ANGER*
Goals

- Reading emotions of anger, in order to explore what is causing the anger.

Instructions for *Matching Empathy to Feelings—Exploring Anger*

1. Start by leading a discussion review of what empathy is.

2. Then explore how anger is expressed in different situations.

3. Ask participants to define how they show anger and when others have shown them anger.

4. Explore also how much anger should or could be tolerated before boundaries need to be set.

5. Discuss what feelings may cause the anger and brainstorm with the group.

6. Create a list of different emotions that may lead to expressing anger.

7. Further explore:

   a. What might that look like?

   b. What are people doing when they are expressing anger?

   c. What does their face look like?

   d. What might their tone sound like?

   e. What might their words be?

8. Create a chart or add to the chart example listed below.

Expressing anger and empathy chart

Feeling of sender	What receiver might be doing	Facial expression of receiver	Tone of receiver	Words of receiver
Active anger (Yelling and getting in personal space with the receiver)	Giving space/listening (Slowly back away from sender)	Calm and concerned	Confident Strong Clear	"I can talk to you about this when you're calm and not yelling." "Please take a minute to calm down and when you're ready, we can talk it out."
Anger (may be accusatory)	Giving space/listening	Calm and concerned	Confident Strong Clear	"It's hard isn't it? Blaming is not going to solve the problem." (Less talking)
Anger moving toward empathy	Getting a little closer and meet eye contact	Calm and concerned	Confident Gentle	"That sounds hard." "Tell me about what happened." (Focused listening)
Anger moving toward empathy	Getting a little closer and meet eye contact	Calm and concerned	Confident Gentle	"What can I do to help?" (Listen and talk about plans only when they are ready)

Repeat steps in Version A, having an observer and a feelings expresser in each pair.

   a. The participant who expresses feelings will choose and express a feeling.

b. The observer will then practice how to respond with facial expressions and body movements only.

c. Leader will then guide the observer to add words to match the empathic body movements and facial expressions.

Example scripts

Active anger

> Sender (yelling and moving in receiver's space): I can't believe my favorite book is gone! I think you stole it—you were looking at it last!

> Receiver (calm and confident): I will talk to you later when you are calm and not yelling.

Anger (may be accusatory)

> Sender (accusatory tone): I can't believe my favorite book is gone! I think you stole it—you were looking at it last...

> Receiver (calm and confident): Wow, I'm sorry you can't find it. Blaming is not going to help solve the problem. In fact, it makes me feel bad and can cause problems in our friendship.

> Sender (calming down and realizing): Oh...you are right. Let me try again. After you looked at it, do you remember where my book went?

Anger moving toward empathy

> Sender: I'm angry, my favorite book is gone. I don't know where it went and I might not be able to finish it before I have to return it.

> Receiver (calm and confident): That sounds difficult. I'm sorry you can't find the book. Do you remember where you last had it?

Wrap up (group discussion)

- What did you feel when you were expressing feelings/showing anger?

- Was it easy/hard to show empathy towards the angry person? What about accepting empathy when angry?

- Why is it important to show empathy during anger?

- How did you feel when the observer demonstrated empathy when you were in anger?

- Who do you typically experience anger from, that you could work on being more empathetic in response to?

Discussing as a whole group, process what they thought about the experience in general.

SUMMARY

Noticing other social cues, such as the environment and the feelings of others, plays a key role in developing and maintaining relationships. This chapter included activities that helped participants better recognize and express their feelings when engaged in social situations. In Chapter 6, we will explore conversation strategies and how to be more present in conversations.

Chapter 6

CONVERSATION STRATEGIES

While it is important to recognize when someone else is not engaging equally in a conversation with us, it is also important to balance recognizing boredom with being able to listen to others. This play demonstrates how others might feel when they are not being listened to and practices the correct way to listen while actually being "present" in the conversation.

YOUR PRESENCE IS A PRESENT

Goals

- Learn how being "present" is a gift.

- Understand why listening is important in a conversation.

- Explore perspectives of self and others about what being "present" means.

Materials needed

- *Your Presence Is a Present* worksheet (see opposite).

- Pencils.

Setting the purpose

Begin by asking participants what "being present" during an interaction with others means. Define it with the group and create a list of examples. Discuss the importance of being present in conversations and how this directly reflects in building healthy relationships, as well as ensuring good discussions with people we meet and work with in general.

YOUR PRESENCE IS A PRESENT

When someone shares in conversation or asks a question it's like giving a present to the other person.

YOUR PRESENCE IS A PRESENT

When someone listens it's like giving a present to the other person. (Thought bubble with present is the thought of the person who is talking.)

A listening present, thank you!!!

Instructions for *Your Presence Is a Present*

1. First model the activity: Have a participant tell you about their weekend.

    a. Demonstrate distracted listening while they speak.

    b. Then, demonstrate "being present" while they speak.

2. Use visuals that demonstrate the leader sharing in conversation with the speaking present bubble. When the listener is listening, show the thinking bubble with a present in it, demonstrating the present that is being given by the listener.

3. When it's the listener's turn to talk, the speaking bubble and thinking bubble will switch to them.

4. Once the concept is demonstrated, have the participants pair up and practice this concept, either one at a time in front or practicing all together.

5. If participants are good at sharing information, it is okay to not use the gift speech bubble. It is okay to just focus on listening as a present, or vice versa.

Wrap up (group discussion)

- How did it feel when others were distracted, and not present in the conversation?

- How did it feel when others were "present" while you spoke?

- When have you felt someone was present for you?

Discussing as a whole group, process what they thought about the experience in general.

PLAY: *YOUR PRESENCE IS A PRESENT*

(Written by Fall 2018 group)

Goals

- To learn, observe, and experience giving and sharing attention.

- Expand on conversion skills and the practice of engaging in 1:1 conversations.

Materials needed

- Cell phone.

- *Your Presence Is a Present* Speech Bubble and Thought Bubble worksheets.

Characters

- Narrator.

- Ryan: Talker.

- Jordan: Who is "listening" wrong.

Scene

Two friends are in a conversation, facing each other.

Ryan and Jordan are in a conversation. Ryan starts talking. Jordan is not listening correctly and at different points, she/he is:

- staring at ceiling

- facing away from Ryan

- looking at cell phone.

Narrator: FREEZE!

What's going on here?

What are Ryan's feelings? (*Not being listened to.*)

Yes, you are right. It made Ryan feel bad and made him/her feel like Jordan didn't want to talk to him/her or maybe that Jordan did not like him/her.

(*Unfreeze the non-listening person*): The right way to listen is for you to look at Ryan, nod, have a nice tone, say nice things like "wow" and "cool", and ask questions!

Sometimes we need a little help on what it looks like to listen. Ryan, can you show us how to listen?

Let's try it again! UNFREEZE!!!

(*Ryan changes places with Jordan and Jordan begins talking. Ryan demonstrates how to listen.*)

Jordan: I like to play video games. Super Mario is my favorite. What do you like to do?

(*Ryan demonstrates good listening by:*

- *Looking; nodding*

- *Saying "Wow!" or "Cool!" (speech bubble with a present on it comes out from the side of face, looking like a speech bubble with the present coming out of the mouth). See "Your Presence Is a Present" worksheet.*

- *Asking a question (present on a stick comes out from the side of face, looking like a present came out of the mouth). See "Your Presence Is a Present" worksheet.)*

Jordan: I like to sing karaoke on the Wii. Do you like to sing?

Ryan: Wow! That's cool. I like to...

The End

Wrap up (group discussion)

- What happened in this play?

- How did Ryan feel?

- If Jordan is bored, is it okay to show he's bored? Why not?

- What can he do instead?

- What are things we can do to show we are listening?

Discussing as a whole group, process what they thought about the experience in general.

WTMI (WAY TOO MUCH INFORMATION)

Building conversation skills

Goals

- Learn how to answer questions, give responses, and disperse information in short form.

- Learn to use small details and stick to the point of the question or conversation.

Setting the purpose

Review basic conversation skills, such as greetings, asking and answering short questions. Review what short conversations are and show examples. Review what "sticking to the point" means and looks like, by showing examples. Leader can show "unexpected" examples as well, to highlight the differences between a long conversation versus a short conversation.

Instructions for *WTMI*

1. Talk about/teach what giving too much information looks like. Show examples through role playing or videos of people that respond to questions with answers that are way too long.

2. Make sure the main topic is understood.

3. Give an "Unexpected" example. Try "How was your weekend?" or any other general question.

    Person 1: How was your weekend?

    Person 2: It was good. I woke up on Saturday morning and wanted to meet my friends at Starbucks. I called Riley, Morgan, and Kelly to meet me there, but only Riley could go. Riley and I decided to get Frappuccinos and a fruit bowl. We then walked to the bridge and fed our leftover fruit to the ducks. Riley accidentally dropped all of the fruit at once into the water, but the ducks seemed to be able to eat it all. We walked downtown and looked at a silly t-shirt store. My favorite t-shirt was of a giraffe and the speech bubble said "Moo." We had a great time.

4. Next give an "Expected" example:

Person 1: How was your weekend?

Person 2: It was great. I met a friend at Starbucks, and we went to the bridge to feed the ducks.

5. Role play expected and unexpected versions of some other sample conversations, then choose two peers to go up in front of a group.

6. Give them a starter question and have each peer take turns responding with "way too much information."

7. Then re-play the scene by asking the same question and respond with a simple answer or sentence.

8. Allow all group members to have a turn, presenting both versions.

9. Allow for constructive criticism or the use of "Hot Sauce" reactions from the audience, as they observe their peers.

Wrap up (group discussion)

- How did it feel being Person 1?

- How did it feel being Person 2?

- What does it feel like giving too much information?

- What does it feel like sticking to the point?

Discussing as a whole group, process what they thought about the experience in general.

TRANSITION WORD ASSOCIATION GAME

In conversation it is important to be able to transition from one topic to another. The *Transition Word Association Game* will help participants practice how to transition to different topics.

Goals

- Increase understanding of transitions in conversation.

- To be able to change the subject or add ideas to conversation in smoother fashion.

Setting the purpose

Oftentimes people like to interject their own topics into conversations. However, bringing up a topic when it is not currently being discussed can be awkward. This word association game can help participants understand how to transition topics.

1. Ask participants: Have you ever had someone in a conversation who really wanted to talk and spoke about an unrelated topic? How did it feel?

2. Choose a participant, have a conversation and in the middle of the conversation, say one of these unrelated sentences or make up your own.

   - "I like turtles and trains."

   - "The rainbow Lucky Charm marshmallow is my favorite."

Instructions for *Transition Word Association Game*

1. Ask a participant for a word.

2. When that participant says a word, write that word down at the top of the board.

3. Ask the next person "What do you think of when you think of his/her word?" Write that person's word under the first word.

4. Keep going until there are at least 20 words or enough to give each person one or two turns.

   Here are some examples of word associations:

Dog	Cooking	Movies
Cat	Rice A Roni	Star Wars
House	Quick meals	Lightsaber
Family	McDonalds	Etc...
Uncle	Friends	

   Example of word association and transition table

Word	Reflection of peer idea, support	Transition
dog	dog	
cat	dog	cat
House	cat	house
Family	house	family
Uncle	family	uncle

cont.

Word	Reflection of peer idea, support	Transition
Cooking	uncle	cooking
Rice A Roni	cooking	Rice A Roni
Quick Meals	Rice A Roni	Quick Meals
McDonalds	Quick Meals	McDonalds
Friends	McDonalds	Friends
movies	Friends	Movies
Star Wars	Movies	Star Wars
Lightsaber	Star Wars	Lightsaber

There are two parts of a transition—reflection and transition. Reflection is an important skill to show listening as well as showing support for a peer, while transitioning with a related topic allows others to know more about the participant.

Lead ins for reflection statements:

- "I like . . . . too."

- ". . . . . are interesting."

- "I don't have any . . . ."

- "Speaking of . . . ."

Transition lead ins:

- "I also like . . . ."

- "But I have . . . ."

5. After the group has their word association, they are to practice a conversation by making a statement for each word, which includes a reflection of what the previous person said as well as transitioning to the next topic. The sentences do not have to be true, as this is practice of how to utilize a reflection statement, as well as a transition topic. It might sound something like this:

   a. My family is thinking about adopting a *dog*.

   b. *Dogs* are amazing animals, but I love *cats*. In fact, I have two cuddly cats!

   c. *Cats* are interesting, but I don't have any at my *house*.

   d. At my *house*, I have a lot of *family* members!

   e. At my house we don't have a lot of *family*, but I love it when I get to visit my *uncle,* he's hilarious.

f. Your *uncle* sounds great! My uncle is a great *cook*.

g. I love *cooking* too, but sometimes we have to resort to *Rice A Roni*.

h. We haven't tried *Rice A Roni*, but we do often have to get a *quick meal* somewhere.

i. Yeah, *quick meals* can be amazing. I love *McDonalds!*

j. *McDonalds* is pretty cool. I like to go there with my *friends*.

k. I love being with my *friends* too. We like to go to the *movies*.

l. Going to a *movie* sounds great. I love going to see *Star Wars*.

m. *Star Wars* is the best. I love playing epic *lightsaber* battles.

Wrap up (group discussion)

Ask these questions to the group:

- How did you feel playing the word association game?

- Was it hard or easy for you to come up with related topics?

- What did you think when we combined our words into a role play with sentences?

- Was it easy or more challenging to combine the topic words with sentences? What made you feel this way?

- How can this be helpful in real conversations?

Discuss as a whole group what they thought about the experience in general.

WHEN I'M STUCK, MAKE THE TOPIC BIGGER!

Goals

- Be able to expand a topic which can help add to a conversation.

Materials needed

- Worksheets: *When I'm Stuck, Make the Topic Bigger* (see overleaf).

Setting the purpose

Everyone has experienced a conversation in which there is a lull where people do not know what to say but might want to continue the conversation. When this happens, it can be helpful to expand on the specific topic being discussed, rather than moving to a more general topic. The leader can say, "We all have gotten into a conversation where we haven't known what to say next. We are going to learn to expand a topic in this activity, which will help us with being able to add more in conversation."

Instructions for *When I'm Stuck, Make the Topic Bigger*

1. Ask the participants to brainstorm topics from a conversation, perhaps a conversation they have felt stuck in. Some example topics are:

   - Frodo, from Lord of the Rings

   - the komodo dragon

   - Acela express train

   - Galaxy S21 android

   - Minecraft zombies.

2. Have participants stand in a circle. Show the worksheet example *When I'm Stuck, Make the Topic Bigger.*

   a. Have one participant read the topic at the bottom.

   b. The next participants expand the topic with reading the next line up on the worksheet example, one person at a time around the circle.

3. Start expanding the topic by using one of the brainstormed topics from the participants *or* from the examples listed above.

4. Next, have participants take turns expanding topics as a group, by going around the circle. You can also pair off the participants, so they can take turns expanding topics in a more formal conversation-based format.

5. Utilize the structure of reflection and transition to move from a narrow to more generalized topic. For example, the conversation practice might go like this:

Person 1: My Maine Coon cat mainly plays fetch with my sister but likes to cuddle with me.

Person 2: My cat is cuddly and likes to play fetch.

Person 3: Cats are the coolest, they are just amazing animals...

Person 4: Dogs and ferrets are great pets too.

Person 5: Pets are wonderful to have.

Person 6: Animals are so interesting.

WHEN I'M STUCK,

MAKE THE TOPIC BIGGER *(EXAMPLE)*

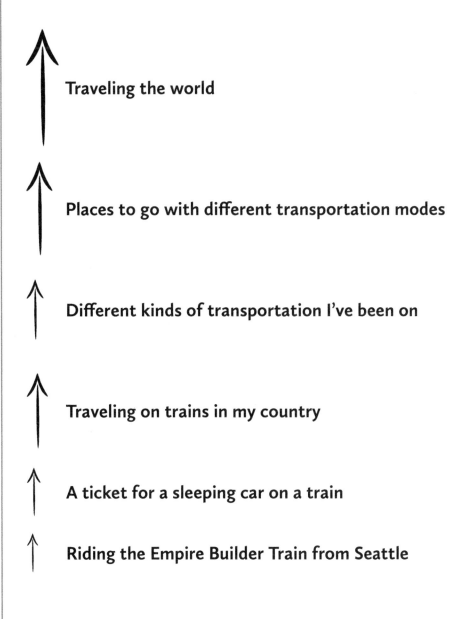

Traveling the world

Places to go with different transportation modes

Different kinds of transportation I've been on

Traveling on trains in my country

A ticket for a sleeping car on a train

Riding the Empire Builder Train from Seattle

WHEN I'M STUCK,

MAKE THE TOPIC BIGGER

↑ ....

↑ ....

↑ ....

↑ ....

↑ ....

↑ ....

As in the sample worksheet, practice transitioning from the word or statement at the bottom, and utilize statements to broaden the conversation all the way to the most general topic.

Note that people may always want to get deeper in their conversation. This might be due to not knowing what to say or feeling shy about taking a risk. Nonetheless, practicing with the following word association game can demonstrate the concept and help participants take a risk without having to share too much if they are not ready.

However, it is important to explain to the participants that taking things to a deeper level is a slower process. If a relationship is newer, the bottom line would not be an appropriate detail to share. Moreover, a conversation might not cover all of these levels, but after having conversations a few times with others it is okay to test the waters and go a level deeper in conversation, but not to go to the deepest level right away.

WHEN I WANT TO GET DEEPER, NARROW THE TOPIC

Goals

- Help participants be able to give a more specific contribution to a conversation, which can help them deepen a relationship.

Materials needed

- Worksheets: *When I Want to Get Deeper, Narrow the Topic* (see next page).

Setting the purpose

Write an extremely general topic at the top of the white board. Then, play a word association game making each next word or phrase a narrower topic. Participants can choose to give real examples of a more detailed experience/thought or a made-up example toward the bottom.

Each person can have a chance to share their story in a sentence, real or made up. Participants should have a chance to share more details after the activity if they would like to.

The leader can say, "If we are in a conversation with someone we feel connected to and want to get deeper in our relationships, we must take risks to share a little more information a little bit at a time. We can start by giving more specific information about our experiences. We are going to practice narrowing a topic in this activity, which will help us with trying to deepen a social connection."

WHEN I WANT TO GET DEEPER,

NARROW THE TOPIC *(EXAMPLE)*

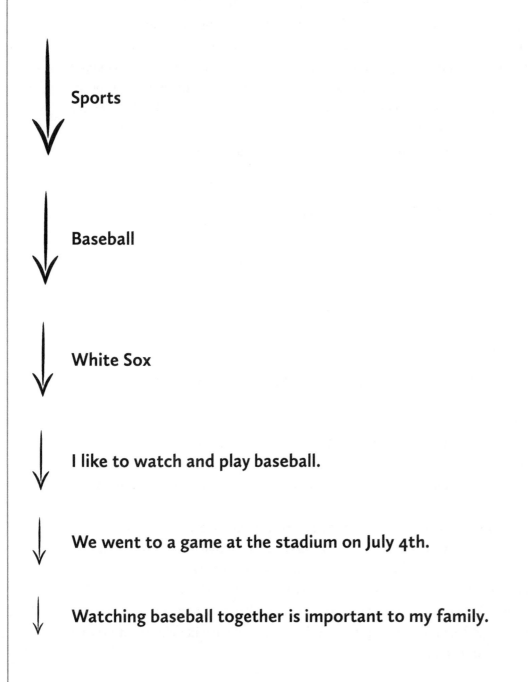

Sports

Baseball

White Sox

I like to watch and play baseball.

We went to a game at the stadium on July 4th.

Watching baseball together is important to my family.

WHEN I WANT TO GET DEEPER,

NARROW THE TOPIC

↓ ....

↓ ....

↓ ....

↓ ....

↓ ....

↓ ....

Instructions for *When I Want to Get Deeper, Narrow the Topic*

1. Ask the participants to brainstorm topics from a conversation, perhaps a conversation they have wanted to continue or deepen. Some examples are:

   - Movies.

   - Books.

   - Electronics.

   - Video games.

2. Have participants stand in a circle. Show the worksheet example *When I Want to Get Deeper, Narrow the Topic*.

   a. Have one participant read the topic at the bottom.

   b. The next participant narrows the topic with reading the next line down on the worksheet example. This continues around the circle.

3. Start a new *When I Want to Get Deeper, Narrow the Topic* word association by starting with one of the brainstormed topics from the participants, or from the examples listed above.

4. Have participants go around the circle to narrow the topics, or if easier have participants take turns narrowing topics in pairs. Utilize the structure of reflection and transition to move from a generalized to more narrow topic. For example, the conversation practice might go like this:

Person 1: I really like sports.

Person 2: I like sports too, baseball is really big in my family.

Person 3: Baseball is important to me too, the White Sox are my team.

Person 4: White Sox are cool. I really love to play baseball but I like to watch it too.

Person 5: We like to watch baseball, and every year we go to the US Cellular Field for Father's Day.

Person 6: I love to go to the White Sox games too, but the last time I went I was so sad when I lost my special necklace.

Wrap up (group discussion)

- How did it feel to share more general topics?

- How did it feel to share more detailed information at the bottom?

- At what level would you feel safe to share with people:

- in your family?

- in your friendship group?

- with this group?

- What makes people not want to share?

- How can you share more details without sharing things that are too personal?

- What would be a motivation to share more details with others?

Discussing as a whole group, process what they thought about the experience in general.

SOCIAL WONDER/WORLD WONDER (VERSIONS A AND B)

Goals

- To be able to recognize a "World Wonder" statement versus a "Social Wonder" statement.

- To strengthen skills of being able to transition from a world wonder topic to a topic that will include social comments, which can help social connectedness.

Introduction to *Social Wonder/World Wonder* Improv (Version A)

Social Thinking addresses the concepts of "Social Wonder" and "World Wonder" in the book *Superflex Takes on One-Sided Sid, Un-Wonderer and the Team of Unthinkables* which is part of the Superflex series by Stephanie Madrigal and Michelle Garcia Winner (2013). Social Wonder and World Wonder are differentiated in the book in order to help the social connection of children through differentiating social interests (Social Wonder) versus facts (World Wonder).

Children, teens, and adults can struggle with discussing facts instead of connecting socially. Thus, the following game has been utilized to help participants notice the difference between facts and social statements and allow practice transitioning facts to social statements.

Setting the purpose

Leader can say, "Sometimes we are interested in different topics that are fact-based or we might be in a conversation with someone who likes to discuss facts. To make a conversation social, we need to learn information about each other, therefore we can practice strategies through this game."

Instructions for *Social Wonder/World Wonder* Improv (Version A)

1. Warm up with using only facts to talk to each other. If participants can't think of any facts, they can make them up. In Improv, everything is accepted.

2. Talk in a voice that would imitate somewhere you would get facts (e.g., Siri, Hey Google, or an encyclopedia type of voice).

3. Then switch to sharing social comments about interests. Made-up interests are accepted here too.

Introduction to *Social Wonder/World Wonder* role play (Version B)

When someone wants to talk about a topic that is a "World Wonder," they might be asking questions or making comments about an aspect of the world or a fact. This does not take us deeper into a friendship. However, when someone has a "Social Wonder," they are curious about others' interests, which they can turn into questions to learn about a person or discuss topics that the other person likes.

Goals

- To be able to recognize a "World Wonder" statement versus a "Social Wonder" statement.

- To strengthen skills of being able to transition from a "World Wonder" topic to a topic that will include social comments, which can help social connectedness.

Materials needed

- One chair for "Social Wonder"; one chair for "World Wonder."

Roles

- Person who only makes "World Wonder" statements.

- Person who replies with "Social Wonder" statements.

Set-up

- Place two chairs next to each other.

- Put a piece of paper on one chair that says "World Wonder."

- Put a piece of paper on the other chair that says "Social Wonder."

Setting the purpose

The leader can say, "Some of us are interested in specific topics and facts about those topics. However, discussing facts too much does not help us learn about others. Learning about others helps us make friends. Therefore, it is important to be able to know the difference between discussing facts and social information. In this activity, we will explore the concepts of 'World Wonder' and 'Social Wonder'."

Instructions for *Social Wonder/World Wonder*

1. Ask one participant to sit in the "World Wonder" chair and one person to sit in the "Social Wonder" chair.

2. The person in the "World Wonder" chair will make statements that are only facts. (The World Wonders facts do not have to be real facts, but can be made up to sound like facts, because in Improv everything is accepted.)

3. In response to the person who makes "World Wonder" statements, the person sitting in the "Social Wonder" chair will respond with "Social Wonder" statements. For example:

   World Wonder: Atari gaming systems were created in 1972, but the first video game console that was made was actually the Magnavox Odyssey.

   Social Wonder: I actually like Atari games, my favorite is Space Invaders.

   World Wonder: Space Invaders was released in 1978, but the original name was not Space Invaders, it was named Space Monsters after a Japanese song.

   Social Wonder: I like to play Space Invaders, but I also really like to play Super Mario Brothers and Minecraft.

Wrap up (group discussion)

- What is the difference between World Wonder and Social Wonder?

- When is it a good time to discuss facts or World Wonders?

- When is it a good time to discuss Social Wonders? With who?

- How did it feel being in the World Wonder role? Social Wonder role?

- Which role can help you develop closer relationships?

Discussing as a whole group, process what they thought about the experience in general.

SUMMARY

Exploring and practicing conversation strategies really helps to strengthen social skills. Being more present in conversations and social interactions also helps maintain developed social skills. In Chapter 7, we expand on being flexible and taking chances. Activities range from storytelling, to putting on a play as a group, and using our imagination to communicate.

Chapter 7

EXPANDING FLEXIBILITY

When someone struggles with flexibility, social struggles are often present. Due to the difficulty of accepting unexpected changes or situations, individuals might have difficulty participating in unexpected routine changes. This could make others feel uncomfortable and limit learning and/or social interaction opportunities.

Being cognitively flexible means having the ability to accept ideas or situations that we did not expect, which in turn allows us to be creative in our problem solving. In Felsman and colleagues' 2020 study, the use of Improv was found to help participants to accept uncertainty and further their divergent thinking skills. Divergent thinking helps to build flexibility, as participants can find connections between concepts that are seen to be unrelated on the surface.

According to Siegel and Bryson (2012), having fun releases dopamine in the brain, which increases motivation in relation to activities, such as social and family relationships. When providing fun activities when learning how to be flexible, you can reward social interactions through the release of dopamine. In the following activities you will find a role play that explores what flexibility and rigidity mean. Moreover, the listed Improv games will help you practice and reward flexible social interactions.

If, by chance, a participant is having difficulty with exploring flexibility, activities can be implemented within the individual's most emotionally safe setting and/or with safe person(s). This could start with the most emotionally safe person, possibly a family member or close friend. As the participant becomes more comfortable, the participant can work with a small group and then possibly a larger group as their comfort level grows.

I'M STUFFED!

A role play about flexible thinking and boxes

Goals

- Increase understanding of rigidity and flexibility.

- Increase ability to problem solve and collaborate within the role play.

Materials needed

- Boxes of different shapes, sizes, and strengths, and/or milk crates.

Setting the purpose

This role play uses the metaphor of boxes to show how our brain organizes things and to highlight what happens if an idea does not fit. Boxes are used to visually show rigidity and flexibility. In the *I'm Stuffed!* exercise, participants need to figure out how to expand their thinking for ideas that do not fit into current boxes. In the second scene, a solution is given, but participants are also encouraged to make up their own solutions to the problem.

The leader can say, "We are going to learn and practice what being rigid and flexible means. Does anyone know what it means to be rigid? What about flexible? Being rigid means being resistant to change or others' ideas. Being flexible is being able to go along with change and others' ideas. We are going to warm up into being flexible and rigid with our bodies first, and then we will read through a play called 'I'm Stuffed'."

Instructions for rigidity and flexibility warm up

1. Have the participants warm up by walking around, demonstrating rigid bodies.

2. The leader can say, "Try to move around with a stiff rigid body."

3. In switching to a flexible body, the leader can state, "Now, change your body to a flexible body and try moving around. How was it trying to move around? Do you think playing basketball would be fun if you and your teammates had rigid bodies? It might be hard to work together if you couldn't bend too well."

Checking for understanding

Ask participants these questions to ensure they understand concepts before moving to the play below.

- What is flexibility?

- What is rigidity?

- What does it look like if we, as people, are rigid? (*A possible answer is getting frustrated with changes, such as in schedules or routines.*)

- What does it look like if we are flexible? (*A possible answer is being able to accept changes and be calm when faced with responses that we don't always want to hear.*)

Next, have the participants look at and explore the boxes in front of them. Have them think of examples of what they put into boxes.

Discussing as a whole group, process what they thought about the experience in general.

Play: *I'm Stuffed!*

Note: Leader should assign the parts of the play to different participants. If there are fewer than nine group members, have a group member play two roles by wearing props to demonstrate different characters.

Roles: (9)

- Narrator.

- Paper box.

- Toy box.

- Art supplies box.

- Rubix cube.

- Video games.

- Construction paper.

- Paper dolls (can be played by one or more people).

- 12-year-old.

Scene 1

Narrator: Boxes hold things. They organize papers, toys, and clothes. It is like how our brains organize thoughts, feelings, ideas, and memories.

Paper box: I hold papers.

Art box: I hold art supplies.

Toy box: I'm a box that holds toys! I hold airplanes, cars, dolls, and stuffies.

Rubix cube: I don't know where to go.

Paper dolls: We don't know where to go.

Construction paper: I don't know where to go. There's not enough room in these boxes... Some of us fit in many boxes. What can we do?

12-year-old (stubbornly folding arms): Hmph. There may not be room, but either way, I don't want to get rid of my things. My dad says this is a mess and I have to organize.

Rubix cube: I can't fit! There's no room in the toy box, aren't I a toy?

Video games: Am I a toy? There's no room in the toy box, I MUST fit in a box!

12-year-old: I don't want to get rid of my toys.

Toy box: I'm stuffed. I have no room and I'm all closed up.

Narrator: FREEZE!

(The leader steps in with the narrator to help process the following questions. The narrator should read the question, but the leader can help the audience participate.)

Narrator: The paper box, toy box, and art supplies box are full and cannot hold any more. The Rubix cube, video games, construction paper, and paper dolls are confused about where they fit in. The 12-year-old does not want to get rid of anything.

Group discussion

- What is happening that is rigid?

- How is this creating an obstacle to solving the problem?

- Would being more flexible help?

- What would that look like to be more flexible?

Narrator: Being flexible and trying to solve problems sometimes can give us a bit of anxiety, as we worry things will not work out in our favor. What can we do to calm ourselves so we can access the parts of our brain that help us problem solve?

(The audience will give suggestions and the actors will all unfreeze and try the suggestions. During practice, the suggestions will come from the actors too.)

Narrator: Now that we have opened our bodies and brains, let's be flexible and find a solution.

At this point, the group should have some ideas on how to resolve the problem in Scene 2. Make sure those ideas are written down. Try the ideas in the next scene. Many ideas can be practiced, and with more practice ideas might merge. Come up with your own group scene. If needed, use the example scene below. Feel free to submit your scene to Socialtheatre.org where your group can be credited and it can be posted on the website!

Next step: Scene 2

Leader will say: Let's demonstrate how the characters (toy box, 12-year-old, video game, toys, art supplies) can be more flexible.

Scene 2 example

Art box, paper box, toy box (Look in own boxes and others' boxes and analyze): Hey, 12-year-old, there are some things inside that are not working. We can make some space.

Rubix cube (Communicate): Toy Box, can you make room for me?

Paper dolls: Art supply box, I might fit with you the best, what do you think?

Construction paper: Paper box, I'm willing to go with you, can you make space for me?

12-year-old: I guess some toys are broken and I don't play with my baby toys.

Video games: I guess the TV shelf could also work.

Toy box: Got rid of baby and broken toys, there's space. If not, sit on top of me.

Everyone: Yay! We figured it out by trying to be flexible.

Variation

Try *I'm Stuffed!* unscripted. At the freeze section, brainstorm ideas and write the ideas on a dry erase board or piece of paper. Have the group try all the ideas or, if there's not enough time, vote on the first two ideas to try and the other ideas can be saved in an idea folder.

Practicing flexibility

In order to practice flexibility, redo the play unscripted, making sure that participants know they are not expected to know the lines, but to make them up according to what they know happened.

When the narrator freezes, explore alternative endings.

How else could this problem end up or be solved? (Then act out the endings.)

Wrap up (group discussion)

First, wrap up this activity by asking participants to choose their favorite flexible body movement or stretch. Once all participants demonstrate their chosen movements to the group, prompt them to sit in a group formation to begin the group discussion.

Then process by asking participants these questions:

- Which ending gave the best solution? Why?

- Which endings needed flexibility?

- Which roles needed to be flexible?

- What was today's lesson about?

- What does flexibility mean?

- What does the opposite, rigid, mean? How are you flexible?

- What does it mean when we say someone might be "rigid" or "flexible"?

FLEXIBLE IMAGINATIONS WITH ONE-WORD STORYTELLING

In this next activity, participants will work on telling a story, one word at a time. While only being able to say one word during each turn can be challenging, it also teaches that relying on the rest of the group can be fun. Even though groups try to create sentences that make sense, oftentimes the sentences are humorous, which takes the stress away and opens up pathways to flexibility.

Goals

- To increase flexibility and ability to accept others' ideas.

Setting the purpose

In one-word storytelling, we do not know where a story will go because the group is telling a story together. Participants will practice their flexibility skills by accepting others' ideas and being present in the moment as they listen to each other's words to make a story.

The leader can say: "We are going to practice our flexibility as we are telling a story one word at a time. Our story will not be what we expect it to be, but will twist and turn in different directions that might or might not make sense. This is part of the fun!"

Instructions for *Flexible Imaginations with One-Word Storytelling*

1. Practice more flexibility of imaginations with one-word storytelling. Remind the group of the Improv rules, to accept others' ideas, and their ideas will be accepted.

2. The group is to stand or sit in a circle.

3. Going around the circle, one person at a time says a word.

4. At the end of a sentence, a group participant is allowed to say "period."

5. Then, a new sentence begins with the next person who says the first word of the new sentence, with each following participant adding a word.

6. The story can be paraphrased or summarized by the leader or a participant at the end.

Challenge

Have the group act out the story.

Wrap up (group discussion)

Discussing as a whole group, process what they thought about the experience in general.

- What was this experience like for you?

- What was an unexpected moment or feeling you had?

- What was your favorite part of the story?

- What might have been uncomfortable, but you were able to get through? (*Possible answer: At one point, I wanted to say a whole phrase or suggest a word to the next person, but I was able to let them have a turn. The story ended up being funny.*)

- How did we get through any discomfort? (*Possible answer: I think hearing the laughter and how funny these stories are helped me accept the process, even though I don't always like that I can't share more than one word.*)

MORPHING CLAY

Goals

- Increase acceptance of others' ideas.

- Build language that demonstrates acceptance of others' ideas.

Setting the purpose

In this activity, participants will be asked to think of something they would like to morph or create out of a ball of pretend clay. The flexibility component comes into play when the participants make the clay into something and give it to the next person, who then has to make an accepting statement.

The leader can say, "We are going to be using a pretend ball of clay to make it into something and give it to the next person."

Instructions for *Morphing Clay*

1. If some participants are having difficulty with flexibility, a warm up to this activity is needed. If the group is already warmed up and flexible, skip to step 2. The warm up would only include participants taking the imaginary ball of clay and morphing it into something they like, naming what it is (e.g., "It's a Rubix cube") and then handing it to the next person who shapes it into something else.

2. In this next level challenge, the participant with the imaginary clay will shape it into something and state what they are giving to the next person (e.g., "I'm giving you a Rubix cube"). The next person takes the imaginary Rubix cube and says, "Thank you," and then morphs the imaginary clay into something else, stating "I'm giving you a . . . ." and passing it to the next person who says "Thank you."

3. In this next level challenge, the participant with the imaginary clay will shape it into something and say what they are giving to the next person (e.g., "I'm giving you a cat"). The next person will take the item and do something with it, and even add words if they want (e.g., "Aw! This cat is so soft and snuggly!" while they are pretending to pet the cat).

4. (*Silly round variation*) The leader will then take a turn and role play with a student who will easily accept something disgusting. The leader will think of something disgusting and say "I'm giving you a . . . . (e.g., skunk)." The participant

receiving the gift (a skunk) will say "Thank you" and add what they will do with the skunk (e.g., "The skunk will act as my brother's alarm clock tomorrow morning!").

Wrap up (group discussion)

- In this activity, how were we being flexible? (*Example: The gifts from others we accepted even if we didn't want to accept them.*)

- What gifts might have been difficult to accept?

- What would have happened to the game if someone didn't accept the gift? (*Example: The game might not have continued and it would not have been as fun anymore.*)

- How did you feel when others accepted the gift and responded to it?

Discussing as a whole group, process what they thought about the experience in general.

ACTING WITH PROPS WITH DIFFERENT PURPOSES

Goals

- Increase flexibility and imagination.

Materials needed

- A pile of random items, feel free to include clown props.

- If participants are in an online meeting, participants can utilize items from their environments.

Setting the purpose
The leader can say, "We are going to use props for unintended purposes, just to be silly. I'll go first to demonstrate." (Then demonstrate using an item for an unintended purpose such as a shoe as a phone.)

Instructions for *Acting with Props with Different Purposes*

1. Tell participants they will choose an item and utilize it for something other than its purpose.

2. The leader will demonstrate first. For example, if the leader has a shoe, it can be used for a phone—the leader can pretend to dial and then talk into the shoe.

3. The participants will each take a turn; feel free to have them exchange or get another prop for the second time around.

Challenge

A challenge could be for another person to respond back with or without their prop, to make a quick Improvisational conversation.

Wrap up (group discussion)

Discussing as a whole group, process what they thought about the experience in general.

- How did you feel about using props as unintended purposes?

- What was good about the activity?

- Was there anything that made you laugh?

FLEXIBLE IMAGINATIONS WITH *YES, LET'S!*

Introduction

In the game *Yes, Let's!* participants get to express their ideas which everyone participates in. This allows everyone to have a chance to express an idea and have it accepted, as well as practice accepting and participating in others' ideas.

Goals

- Increase turn taking and idea acceptance between group members.

Setting the purpose

The leader can say, "We are going to play a game that allows *all* of your ideas to be accepted. When our ideas are accepted by others, it feels good. We are going to share our ideas and help each other feel good with this activity."

Instructions for *Yes, Let's!*

1. The first person comes up with an idea of an action, saying, "Let's . . . ." (e.g., "Let's go skydiving!").

2. Everyone responds with "Yes, let's!" and then pretends to do the action.

3. The next person then gets a turn to give an idea to which everyone responds with "Yes, let's!" and then participates in the action.

4. Repeat the process until everyone gets a turn to send out an idea and action.

Wrap up (group discussion)

Discussing as a whole group, process what they thought about the experience in general.

- How did this activity feel to you?

- What part of the activity was fun? Challenging?

- How did it feel to have your idea accepted and acted out?

- How did others feel when you acted out their ideas?

SUMMARY

Participating together in activities that reinforce the acceptance of one's ideas, as well as returning the acceptance, can increase the reward of flexible social interaction. As Felsman and colleagues' (2020) study found, Improv can increase acceptance of uncertainty and "promotes divergent thinking". To understand different relationship roles and behavior, it is important to be flexible in one's thinking, as relationships do not always fit into a category. The next chapter will give some guidelines about how one can respond in different relationship roles.

Chapter 8

DEFINING RELATIONSHIP ROLES

When trying to understand our relationships to others, it is important to be able to notice cues as to who is closer and who is more distant. Being able to distinguish a relationship's closeness can help in knowing what might be appropriate to discuss or even know how to handle responding to an unexpected situation, such as a person wearing clown shoes.

LEVEL OF RELATIONSHIPS AND BEHAVIOR

When discussing levels of relationships, one must consider the various types of relationships, along with the related behaviors associated with those specific relationships. Although this can evolve into a complicated series of lessons, the use of sketch comedy can help simplify examples within these lessons, by demonstrating the various types of relationships in real time. Having the option of seeing and participating in the scenes further strengthens the participants' understanding of the relationship presented as well. For example, when talking about the difference between a best friend and a good friend, the differences can be subtle. When placing this lesson into a scene, one can observe or experience those subtle differences in real time, allowing for a deeper understanding of the relationship presented.

In order to help participants to understand relationships, it is important to know how they can be defined. This guide shows ways in which participants can deepen relationships through developing trust as well as helping them to develop understanding about which conversations are appropriate at different stages of relationship. The following activity and accompanying play demonstrate how someone on a specific relationship level can respond to another person who might display "unexpected behavior," such as wearing clown shoes.

Sometimes we feel uncomfortable about giving a compliment on things we don't like, and it could come off as ingenuine. Therefore, it is important to learn not to say anything or, if with someone in a closer relationship, how to hint. With a family member, it might even be okay to be direct.

PROCESSING: WHAT ARE RELATIONSHIPS AND WHY ARE THEY IMPORTANT?

It is important to gauge the interest and knowledge of your participants when it comes to relationships. Humans are mostly designed as social creatures. This means we need others to survive and thrive. If we isolate ourselves, it may increase the chances of feeling lonely, which may lead to depression. However, being around others and having positive interactions helps to release oxytocin and dopamine, which helps feelgood chemistry occur in our brains (Hung *et al.,* 2017). Process the participants' feelings about relationships by asking the following questions:

- What are relationships? (They can be social, family, romantic, work or school.)

- Why are relationships important?

- Why do we need different types of relationships?

IMPROVISING A RELATIONSHIP

Goals

- Increase awareness of different types of relationships and behavior.

Setting the purpose

The leader can state, "We all have different types of relationships in our lives. We act differently when we are with our dentist versus with a parent; we also act differently when we are with a friend versus a sibling. In some relationships we can share more of our feelings and deeper information. With our dentist, we would not share something embarrassing that happened, but we might tell a sibling or parent. With a friend from school, we would not tell them that we are about to go take a shower, but we might share that with a family member who lives at our house."

Instructions for *Improvising a Relationship*

1. Brainstorm types of relationships and write them on a whiteboard or piece of paper.

2. Two people at a time can choose a relationship type without telling the rest of the group, and role play the relationship.

3. The other participants will guess what relationship type or level the Improvisers acted with each other.

4. Ask questions at the end of each role play:

   - What were the cues that gave you an idea that they were this relationship type?

   - What was their body language, space, and tone of voice like?

- What details in their words told you about their relationship?

Wrap up (group discussion)

- How did you feel about Improvising relationships?

- What was easy? More challenging?

- Was it more challenging to Improvise a relationship or to figure out what relationship? What makes you feel that way?

- What relationships were easier to read? Which relationships showed more similarities which might have made reading them more difficult?

DEFINING RELATIONSHIPS

Goals

- Demonstrate relationship levels through role playing specific relationships.

Setting the purpose

The leader can say, "In our relationships, we can talk and share more with those who are closer to us, such as a sibling or a parent. However, we do not share anything with those we do not know, such as a stranger. For those relationships with people we know a little, such as with an acquaintance from school or work, we can share a little. We can share more with those we know better, such as a friend we sit with for lunch at work or school. In this activity, we are going to define relationship roles and what they mean, as well as practice what it might look like if we saw a person walking."

Instructions for *Defining Relationships*

1. Ask participants to role play each of the following categories.

2. First, have participants utilize the scripts.

3. After reading the scripts, have the participants come up with their own interaction without scripts, based upon that relationship level.

Stranger
A stranger has no contact with or need for recognition of each other. If it is a recognizable face of someone from the community, a head nod is okay.

Person 1: Hi. (*walks with purpose, quick eye contact to say hi or nod, not stopping or slowing*)

Person 2: Hi. (*responds with quick eye contact and hi or not, not stopping or slowing*)

Acquaintance

Acquaintances might have conversations with someone because of a situation or circumstance (e.g., they are waiting in the hallway with you).

ACQUAINTANCE LEVEL SCRIPT

Walking in the same direction, exiting the gym with someone who was at the basketball game too. The pair were not sitting together and might or might not know each other's names and faces. They are of similar age.

> *Person 1*: That was a close game!
>
> *Person 2*: Yeah, I didn't expect that three-pointer.
>
> *Person 1*: I can't wait to see them play Notre Dame.
>
> *Person 2*: That should be a good one. Maybe see you there.
>
> *Person 1*: Okay, bye.

A SECOND ACQUAINTANCE LEVEL SCRIPT

Walking towards each other on the sidewalk, they know each other's names from a common setting such as school, work, or group activities. They have somewhere to go or are not yet feeling ready to engage in a deeper conversation due to relationship level. However, with one of the next conversations, more information can be shared which can eventually get deeper.

> *Jake*: (*Some eye contact, slowing down to exchange friendly greetings.*) Hi, Ben, how are you?
>
> *Ben*: Jake, good to see you. How are you?
>
> *Jake*: I'm fine. Are you going to the Fall fest later?
>
> *Ben:* Yes, maybe I'll see you there.
>
> *Jake*: Yes, see you there. Bye.

Social friend

At this relationship level, friends are those who share a setting, choose to spend time together in this setting, and might make plans to hang out at other times. When getting closer, these friends might choose to begin planning and spending time together outside of shared settings.

A SOCIAL FRIEND SCRIPT

> *Riley*: Hi, Abby, it was fun bowling with you on Friday.
>
> *Abby*: Hi, Riley, it was fun! I thought we did pretty good this time.

Riley: I don't know about that gutter ball, but we pulled it together.

Abby: It was hilarious when I dropped the ball when it was quiet.

Riley: That was pretty funny, but happens to all of us. I wish we would have had time to check out the arcade.

Abby: I like to go to the arcade too, but I also like video games and playing with friends.

Riley: We have a Nintendo Switch, I like to play Mario Brothers and Animal Crossing.

Abby: We should play video games next time we hang out, although I do like a game of air hockey at the arcade too.

Riley: Yes to both, but for now let's get our friends together this weekend and we can all go to the arcade.

Abby: Okay! Friday? I'll send a group text.

Best friend

Best friends are those who spend time together, plan time to be together, and have each other's backs. They also might deepen their relationship into being lifelong friends who share hopes, dreams, and secrets.

BEST FRIEND SCRIPT

Amanda: Hi Momo! (*Hug or secret handshake.*)

Morgan: Hi Mandy!

Amanda: It was so funny yesterday when you were at the table laughing and milk came out of your nose.

Morgan: Omg. I couldn't contain myself. Your crossed eyes, they get me every time!

Amanda: And, your brother laughing...

Morgan: With him laughing too, it was too much.

Amanda: Momo, I see that look you are giving me. Okay, I know he annoys you.

Morgan: He is annoying. I knew what you were thinking when you gave me that look. You are thinking I'm being dramatic.

Amanda: Yes! Just enjoy your time with your brother. After all, he is pretty funny...

Siblings

Although siblings are not typically defined as friendships, we felt it is important to demonstrate the difference in how blatantly honest siblings can typically be. In addition, siblings offer a deeper level of connection that can allow for more meaningful communication.

Meanwhile siblings can also have an easier path to conflict, which is typical for a sibling relationship.

SIBLING SCRIPT

> *Morgan*: Why do you have to be around when my friends are over? It's annoying.
>
> *Eric*: You are annoying. But…I like your friends.
>
> *Morgan*: Get your own friends. Hang out with Aiden or something.
>
> *Eric*: Dork! You know I have friends, I just like to be with you too.
>
> *Morgan*: Ugh. I know… Okay, just don't be annoying.

Setting the purpose

The leader can state, "In our relationships, we are expected to be able to share deeper feelings and thoughts with those who are closer to us, but for those who aren't as close we are not expected to share deep feelings. When someone wears something we think looks goofy or out of place, our relationships define how open we can be about our thoughts about what they are wearing. This includes other times that we might not approve of something that does not affect us, such as a person's behavior. These things do not directly affect us, such as the book series they choose to talk about, how they choose friends that we don't have anything in common with, or when they might enjoy the spotlight a little too much."

To keep the activity fun and easier to learn the concept, make sure to mainly use examples about appearance, although the concept can be utilized in later discussions about relationship levels and how to approach interactions about the behavior of others.

Relationship roles and response worksheet: *Interesting Shoes*

Before trying the play with the group, discuss the different levels of relationships and what you would expect out of these relationships. The sections below helps discuss how one would act around a person within a relationship level, who is for example wearing clown shoes. An empty grid worksheet follows overleaf for use during lessons.

Strangers

A stranger has no contact with or need for recognition of each other. If it is a recognizable face of someone from the community, a head nod is okay.

Example: See a random person with clown shoes, briefly look at them and then look away again.

Acquaintance

Acquaintances might have conversations with someone because of a situation or circumstance (e.g., they are waiting in the hallway with you).

Example: Acknowledge the person with the clown shoes by saying hi and not saying anything about the shoes.

Social friend

At this relationship level, friends are those who share a setting, choose to spend time together in this setting, and might make plans to hang out at other times. When getting closer, these friends might choose to begin planning and spending time together outside of shared settings.

Example: Having basic exchanges of conversation (hello, how are you and reciprocate) with another topic of interest, followed by noticing they got new shoes or not saying anything.

Best friend

Social Thinking® splits this category into two levels—bonded friend and close friend. Bonded friends spend time together, plan time to be together, and have each other's backs. Close friends, according to *Socially Curious and Curiously Social* (Garcia Winner and Crooke, 2011), are lifelong friends who share hopes, dreams, and secrets. For the purpose of this activity, we are using "best friend" to demonstrate someone who will try to be honest but nice.

Example: Acknowledge the person with the clown shoes by saying hi, asking them why they are wearing those shoes, and then asking what led to them choosing to wear the shoes.

Sibling

Although Social Thinking® does not include siblings as a friendship level, we felt it is important to demonstrate the difference in how bluntly honest a sibling can typically be. In addition, we wanted to acknowledge that siblings offer a deeper level of connection that allows for more meaningful communication.

Example: Acknowledge the sibling and then ask them why they are wearing those shoes and then maybe make fun of them for wearing them.

INTERESTING SHOES

A play and activity about responses within different relationship levels

> Identify small unexpected behavior
>
> Wearing clown shoes   Wearing a pretend mustache
>
> Talking loudly on the phone   Wearing clothes backward
>
> Other: . . . .

Relationship type or level	Response
Stranger	
Acquaintance (Know each other's names and sometimes say hi)	
Social friend (Have hung out during unstructured times or outside of school)	
Best friend (Keeps secrets/ spend time at each other's houses/phone calls daily)	
Sibling	

Questions to consider

- What reactions would you have to a person who wears clown shoes?
- Would you mention it?
- Would you pretend you didn't see?
- If you do talk about the clown shoes, what would be acceptable to say?

The following worksheet is an example of what responses could be appropriate, given relationship level.

Relationship type	Response
Strangers	Walk past and don't say anything. May notice shoes, but without other person seeing them look (a subtle glance with small eyebrow raise or no reaction).
Acquaintance	Hi, how is your day going? Mine is good too, I'm just on my way to science. See you later.
Social friends	Say, "Hi! How are you doing?" Have a few conversation exchanges about interests and say "I see you got new shoes."
Best friend	Say "Hi! How are things? I've been great too, went shopping. Speaking of shopping, did you get new shoes? They are interesting. I really liked the blue shoes you had."
Sibling	"Wow, those shoes are ridiculous. No offense, brother. I don't want you to be socially outcasted."

With your group, utilize the worksheet on the previous page to brainstorm responses of how you might respond to those within each relationship level. Utilize the responses your group has formed, or the examples above, for the play.

As well as the clown shoes example, other possibilities include:

- Wearing a *huge* mustache.

- Wearing a shirt backwards.

- Carrying a teddy bear when you're old enough that it's unexpected.

- Talking too loud on the cell phone.

- Make up your own example.

PLAY: INTERESTING SHOES AND RELATIONSHIP RESPONSE

(Written by Social Theatre Fall 2018 group)

Goals

- To develop and recognize response in relationship roles.

- Recognize different types of relationships.

Materials needed

- Print out the worksheet *Relationship Roles* overleaf to make visuals by punching out the holes and adding yarn to make signs for each actor.

- Completed *Interesting Shoes* form from previous page.

- A pair of silly shoes or other silly costume item.

Instructions for *Interesting Shoes*

1. Choose which participant will wear the clown shoes.

2. In the play, each actor will alternate roles by wearing one sign. The participant wearing the clown shoes will not have a sign.

3. If there are not enough participants, participants can take on the role of more than one character.

4. Participants will walk toward each other as if passing on the sidewalk in their neighborhood.

RELATIONSHIP ROLES FOR
INTERESTING SHOES PLAY

Punch holes in the top corners and thread a string around in order for the signs to be worn.

Stranger

Acquaintance

Social Friend

Best Friend

Sibling

Play set up: *Interesting Shoes*
Characters

- Narrator.

- Stranger.

- Acquaintance.

- Social friend.

- Best friend.

- Sibling.

- Person wearing clown shoes, or other prop/idea.

Act 1

Narrator: How does a person communicate with someone who is wearing ridiculous clown shoes? Well...it depends on the relationship. We are going to demonstrate the difference depending on the relationship.

(Person with clown shoes/or mustache walks from one side of the room, while a stranger walks toward and past the person with the clown shoes. They give the "stranger" response that the group filled in on the grid. Next, the person with clown shoes walks back across the room while the acquaintance walks toward the person with clown shoes and in passing, they give the "acquaintance" response the group chose previously. Next, the social friend and person with clown shoes walk toward each other, and the social friend responds according to the group's chosen response. When the best friend and person with clown shoes walk toward each other they respond as agreed by the group. Lastly, the sibling and person with clown shoes walk toward each other and the sibling offers the agreed response.)

Act 2

The narrator leads a discussion with the audience about the different responses.

(Afterwards, for closure and routine, have all actors stand in a line and bow.)

Wrap up (group discussion)

- What was the focus of these activities?

- What social cues did you have to pay attention to?

- What conversation skills were you using for these activities?

- What types of relationships did you recognize?

- What types of relationships do you have in your life?

- What are your most important relationships? How direct can you be in those relationships?

Discussing as a whole group, process what they thought about the experience in general.

Closing exercise options

- Choose a favorite moment of the day. Everyone takes a turn to share with the group.

- Create a circle. Each person will choose one "take away" from the day to throw in the middle of the circle. They will take turns saying it and then making the hand motion of throwing it in the middle of the circle.

SUMMARY

In summary, relationship roles are important when distinguishing how to respond and converse with those in our lives. Interacting with those who are closer in a relationship allows us to be more direct, whereas we might not want to talk about something that could be awkward (such as wearing clown shoes) with those we are not close to. By gaining a deeper understanding of why we should look at relationship roles, we gain the ability to see the perspective of others. With perspective taking, we can understand that others who are not close to us, or do not have a deeper level of trust with us, may not feel safe with direct comments about what they are wearing. In the next chapter, activities will help practice and deepen perspective-taking skills.

Chapter 9

PERSPECTIVE TAKING

Taking perspectives is one of the most difficult tasks for a human to do. It is especially difficult for those struggling with social/emotional issues, in which not taking perspectives is what causes most of their difficulties with social interactions. Practicing taking different perspectives, even if we do not agree with them, really helps loosen up views and encourages flexibility in communication. This is also very important in developing healthy relationships with people and in turn developing our own personal perspectives with confidence.

SWITCHING PERSPECTIVES

Goals

- To practice being able to see and discuss another perspective than one's own.

Setting the purpose

One typically feels more confident when discussing topics that are familiar to them. However, when discussing topics that are unfamiliar, confidence may be lost. These feelings of uncertainty can lead to stress or anxiety.

The group leader can say, "We are going to brainstorm your topics of interest and topics that you might not be interested in. It will be fun to see what everyone's interests are, and what can be challenging is to relate to topics that we may not be interested in. After we brainstorm, we will practice perspective taking with these topics."

Instructions for *Switching Perspectives*

1. Everyone writes down all the topics they are interested in on the board.

2. Have each person circle three topics: one topic they are interested in, another topic they don't know about or are neutral about, and one topic they are uninterested in.

3. Have them choose which two topics to ramble about.

4. Participants can then take a turn rambling in support of the two topics, meaning talking without spaces or pauses.

Challenge

Take out the neutral choice, only have participants choose a topic they are most interested in and topic they are least interested in.

Wrap up (group discussion)

Discussing as a whole group, participants can process what they thought about the experience in general.

- How was your experience rambling?

- What did you think about rambles from those who were not interested in your favorite topics?

  - Do you think it was easy or challenging for them?

- For you, which ramble was easiest? Most challenging?

  - Why do you think it was this way?

TESTING PERSPECTIVES

Goals

- Listening to perspectives different from one's own.

- Respect others' perspectives, even though one's own perspective is different.

Setting the purpose

Review advanced conversation skills, such as asking and answering questions and getting to know a person on a deeper level. Review what long conversations are and show examples. Review asking and answering questions, sharing opinions, and respecting differences of opinion. Leaders can show "unexpected" examples as well, to highlight the differences between respectful and genuine conversations versus uncomfortable conversations.

Instructions for *Testing Perspectives*

1. The leader starts by making a list of opinions participants have about non-personal random subjects that do not include politics or religion. Examples: "I hate pickles because they are too bitter," or "I love dogs because they are loyal."

2. Everyone needs to give out at least one opinion.

3. Be sure to initial the opinions, so that leaders can keep track of who wrote what, so that participants are not supporting their own opinion(s).

4. Assign opinions to participants.

5. Each participant will go up in front of the group and present the opinion in a believable way. Once all have presented, group members will be aware of what each is supporting.

6. The group will then be split off into pairs and asked to speak to each other about those options, as if it were their own true perspective.

7. Allow time to participate and chat.

8. Stop the exercise and process the experience as a group.

Wrap up (group discussion)

- What did it feel like taking another person's perspective?

- What was their perspective?

- Do you agree or disagree with the opinion?

- Were you able to accept the perspective by the end of the experience? Or are you still against it?

- Are you able to better understand your group member(s)?

Discussing as a whole group, process what they thought about the experience in general.

Expand

Discussion can continue into how group members can generally respect each other, as well as the people in their lives, even when they have very different opinions and perspectives. Examples include family members, friends, co-workers, politicians, celebrities, teachers, bosses/managers, authority figures, or social media figures.

STEP INTO MY MIND

Goals

- To listen to participants' perspectives and figuratively step into their mind.

- To respect others' perspectives and build empathy by experiencing what they are feeling.

Setting the purpose

Discuss empathy and how it applies in this activity, when the participant is mimicking their partner's feelings through body movements and facial expressions. Also discuss how to pick up on what caused the feelings and physical body expressions to happen in the first place. Discuss why it is important to understand what others feel and why, and how that might contribute to their expressions and reactions.

Instructions for *Step into My Mind*

1. The leader begins by assigning pairs.

2. The pairs choose who will mimic and who will lead.

3. The leading partner is then given a feeling to express, based on a specific scenario. The leader must use their face and body as much as possible.

4. The mimicking partner will follow, finding themselves fused in the movements and scene.

5. Switch sides and play it out again, using a different feeling and scenario.

Example scenarios

• Feeling happy about a new purchase.

• Feeling sad about the loss of a pet.

• Feeling mad about losing something valuable.

• Feeling confused about what to wear.

• Feeling surprised at their surprise birthday party.

Wrap up (group discussion)

• What did it feel like taking another person's perspective?

• How did it feel using the same facial expressions and body movements as your partner?

• When exactly did you feel the way that they were feeling?

Discussing as a whole group, process what they thought about the experience in general.

SUMMARY

Taking and testing perspectives really helps in expanding flexibility in communication. It also helps deepen social interactions and strengthen communication skills. Social interaction involves a lot of flexibility and taking into account the other person's perspective. Good conversations that have purpose will ultimately increase the confidence of the participants, while also strengthening relationships. In Chapter 10, we move into developing the inner monologue, practicing coping skills, and introducing the concept of mindfulness. Activities focus on building confidence, staying open-minded and positive, and being more aware of the environment and surroundings you are in.

DEVELOPING THE INNER MONOLOGUE, COPING SKILLS, AND MINDFULNESS

The basic premise of assertiveness is speaking with confidence and speaking up for oneself (based on "Superhero" play from Spring 2019 Social Theatre™). In this chapter we focus on developing that inner monologue that supports us in being confident and advocating for ourselves when needed. The skill of thinking positively and asking for help when needed can be a difficult one because it needs constant practice.

THE EMPOWERMENT SHIELD

Goals

- Developing positive personal slogans as a personal shield. Slogans should empower, build, and strengthen confidence.

- Expanding on developing and strengthening coping skill(s).

Materials needed

- Art and craft materials: cardboard, poster board, markers, crayons, colored pencils, glue, paper, stickers, magazine pictures, cutouts.

Setting the purpose

Review what a personal and empowering slogan is. Review what empowerment means and how to empower ourselves and others with slogans. The leader can show examples of slogans already in use in social media, such as "Keep Calm and Carry On" and "Stay Strong." Highlight which slogans empower others and which empower them personally.

Note: Clinical Application. Creating a shield with slogans/words is similar to the use of "Positive Self-Talk," which derives from cognitive behavior therapy (CBT) applications.

It can be applied in the process of confidence building, assertiveness training, and building self-advocacy skills.

Instructions for making *The Empowerment Shield*
Children/Teens

1. Create a small list of the negative talk or the common threads of negativity they experience in their life.

2. Once complete, work together in developing a slogan or slogans that are inspiring to them.

3. Next, create a "shield" from the negative vibes/words/actions that are coming toward them. Do this by writing the positive words/slogan(s) on the exterior of the shield. Decorate the exterior of the shield with the words/slogans chosen.

Adults

1. Follow the instructions for children/teens *or* it can be completed metaphorically—by writing on a list. This version of the list contains their name and two columns. Column 1: Negative Slogan(s) Column 2: Positive or "Shield Slogan."

2. Then go around the group and process the lists.

3. Finally, create the physical representation of the "Shield."

   If a participant chooses not to complete building an actual shield, they can write it out on a piece of paper instead. This can be done on a hand-drawn shield shape of their choice *or* using a free template online. They would then write out the slogan(s) and embellish it, if they choose.

Instructions for *The Empowerment Shield* Improv

1. Have participants stand in a circle.

2. Participants will say their slogan out loud, which will be repeated around the circle. Everyone will get to state their slogan, which will be repeated around the circle.

3. The next time, the participants will add an action to say with their slogan, which will also be repeated and enacted around the circle.

4. *Optional:* The third time around the circle, add a massive amount of exaggeration to the slogan's action.

The Shield game
Note: This game should be played in slow motion in much smaller groups, or even one at a time for those who struggle with physical self-regulation.

1. First, have participants brainstorm and write a list on one side of the board of positive, encouraging slogans. The other side of the board is for negative comments that refute those slogans creating a back and forth between negative and positive thinking. *To maintain boundaries, these words on the board should be the only ones used during the enactment.*

2. Set up the two sides of the playing area/stage. One side is the negative side, the other is the positive side. (Everyone should take turns being on each side.)

3. Practice the battle stance with an emphasis on *slow motion*, charging movements, and blocking poses. The leader can role play big expressions with slower more expressive controlled movement and with no actual touching, just using body control to make it appear there has been physical contact and reactions.

4. The leader will position everyone. They will then begin the scene by simply saying the cue word: "Charge"!

5. Optional music can be added to the sequence, such as battle music from movie scores or video games. Leader should encourage battle cries within the group (e.g., Forge on!! Gooooo!!).

6. Once they get into the middle of the stage area, they will be told to stop charging, then start shouting the positive slogans and negative slogans at the same time. *Or the group can synchronize the shouting, where one person shouts out a negative slogan and the other side shouts the positive.*

7. Encourage fake battle movements of "shielding", so they shield from negative slogans from the negative side, as the positive words are being thrown back (e.g., using the shield to push back). Example negative slogans are yelled out and depicted figuratively as "cannon balls" flying over from one side. The positive side/receivers are deflecting them with their hands and shields, while yelling back the positive slogans.

Variation and additional layers
Child/Teens
Encourage them to take the actual shield, hold it up, and use it figuratively against the rest of the group.

Additional activity: *Use the Shield!!!* play
Characters

- Wolfboy.

- Icegirl.

- Dr. Evil.

- Narrator.

Materials

- Use shield created from the above activity and draw a speech bubble on a piece of paper with the phrase MEAN WORDS! written on it.

Setting
School+Lair under the school

> *Narrator:* Welcome to superhero school. Today we are observing Wolfboy and Icegirl's power. Wolfboy and Icegirl both have distinct powers to ward off Evil. Let's discover what they are.

> *Dr. Evil (to Wolfboy):* I'm going to get you, and take away all of your power. I'm going to destroy you with my Evil, Mean Words! (*Dr. Evil holds up a speaking bubble with "MEAN WORDS" written on it.*) Mean Words! Mean Words!

> (*Wolfboy is doubling over and being affected by Dr. Evil's mean words.*)

> *Narrator:* FREEZE!!

> (*Brainstorm how the group wants to show they are being affected by these words. What emotions would they feel? What and how do they want to demonstrate? How do we want the audience to view it? What lesson are we trying to teach?*)

> *Narrator:* What is happening here? What is Dr. Evil trying to do? Why? What is Wolfboy feeling? What can help the situation? How should this problem be solved? ... Those are great ideas! Icegirl has an idea. (*Bring out Icegirl.*) Icegirl, what do you think should be done to prevent Dr. Evil from gaining power over Wolfboy?

> *Icegirl:* Wolfboy can't let Dr. Evil take his power! I'll help him out by showing him my shielding strategy. It works by shielding me from "Mean Words" and does not let these words take power from me. This way, I still feel good about myself!

> *Narrator:* Okay, show us how it's done! UNFREEZE!

> (*Wolfboy is still cowering to Dr. Evil's power—his mean words. Icegirl steps in and demonstrates how to use the shield. Dr. Evil's words get closer to the shield and bounce off. Dr. Evil gives up on Icegirl and tries again with Wolfboy. Wolfboy turns into a stuffed wolf by turning around a couple times fast and leaving a stuffed wolf onstage (running offstage). Dr. Evil then completely changes character as he walks over to the stuffed wolf, cuddles and talks baby talk to the stuffed wolf.*)

> *Wolfboy (from backstage):* Yuck. That's enough. I'm changing back!

> *Wolfboy (comes back on stage, as the stuffed animal is thrown off stage):* Dr. Evil, I am not letting you take my power!

> *Dr. Evil:* Well then, until next time! (*Exits stage with evil laugh.*)

> The End

Wrap up (group discussion)

- What did it feel like creating your slogan?

- Do you get inspired by other people's slogans?

- Which ones inspired you most?

Discussing as a whole group, process what they thought about the experience in general.

FINDING OUR INNER SUPERHERO

Goals

- Finding our personal inner voice of support while addressing a myriad of feelings.

- Practice and learn how to use the supportive voice in defending against inner and outer negativity.

Setting the purpose

Even superheroes have a myriad of feelings. All of us also have a superhero in us, we just have to find them and lure them out. Pay close attention to the characteristics of what make up this character, as they will also define us. Characteristics can be viewed as different personality traits that define a person, the choices they make, and their behaviors. We are going to play these roles to make sure they are a good fit and make any adjustments needed.

Instructions for *Finding Our Inner Superhero*

1. Determine a character, such as a superhero.

2. Brainstorm what parts of that character make up the whole person. (Example: brave Wonder Woman, scared Wonder Woman, annoyed Wonder Woman, shy Wonder Woman, etc.)

3. Each participant chooses a part to play.

4. Each person takes turns saying one sentence in accordance with what their character trait would say.

5. As participants feel comfortable, they can dialogue with the other character traits staying in their own character.

Wrap up (group discussion)

- What part do you relate to most? Why?

- What part do you want to relate to more? Why?

- Why are these parts important?

Discussing as a whole group, process what they thought about the experience in general.

The following play is developed for the purpose of encouraging the practice of social emotional skills such as working together, using a coping strategy and the power of positive thinking. These plays will also help in supporting the practice of role plays and further enhance practicing various social skills and pro-social behaviors. Some of these plays were developed during Social Theatre™ workshops.

DR. EVIL'S REMOTE CONTROL

A play about negative thinking

(Written by Social Theatre Fall 2018 group)

Roles

- Dr. Evil.

- Kid 1.

- Kid 2.

Act 1

Dr. Evil (holding remote control): I'm Dr. Evil and I'm going to control the universe. This special brain remote will help me control people so I can own them and everything they have! Hah hah hah.

I just have to put negative thoughts in their head that everything will go wrong! And, guess what? It will!

I see that these kids are thinking about their difficult time building LEGO®s. Hippocampus, remind them all about their bad memories and failures about building things!

I'm pressing the Hippocampus Bad Memories button right NOW!

Act 2

(Kids are separately trying to build with boxes.)

Kid 1: I am never going to get this built. There's too many to even think of.

Kid 2: I know the last time I was building like this, a kindergartener came and knocked everything down. It always gets destroyed.

Kid 1: And you know what? Last time, no one even came to help. I was trying to get it done all by myself and I didn't even know how to do it.

(Kid 1 and Kid 2 stop working and sit with their chins in their hands.)

Act 3

Dr. Evil: See? It's working. They will never get their things done and I will control the world. They have lost hope, hahaha!

(*Kid 1 and Kid 2 trying to regain control as they are holding their heads. Meanwhile Dr. Evil is having difficulty with remote and getting frustrated with malfunctioning remote.*)

Dr. Evil: Arggg!!! I am losing!

Kid 1 (gets a drink of water): Wow, that must have been a magic potion, it cleared up my brain!

Kid 2 (exhales out): My brain just cleared up too!

(*Dr. Evil in the background trying to figure out why the remote isn't working.*)

Kid 1 and Kid 2: So, how are we going to be able to finish this?

Dr. Evil: No! Don't work together! If you do, I can't control the world!

(*Kid 1 and Kid 2 finish the tower together.*)

The End

Wrap up (group discussion)

- How did it feel watching Dr. Evil?

- How did it feel for the players, playing the roles?

- How was the experience for the audience members?

- If you could change something that Dr. Evil did, what would it be?

- If you could change something the kids did, what would it be?

MINDFULNESS ACTIVITIES

This section focuses on activities that support mindfulness. Mindfulness is very important because it helps build focus and awareness. When utilizing mindfulness, we learn to be in the moment, accepting outside thoughts while also refocusing. In our ability to refocus our thoughts, we are more able to build stamina for focused thinking.

MINDFULNESS MOMENT OF EMPOWERMENT

Let's practice being in the moment. Let all outside thoughts drift away, and as they come back in, imagine them floating back out as you refocus on the moment. Take a deep breath, exhaling any stress or any thoughts besides this moment. Take a moment to repeat your empowerment slogan or an encouraging message to yourself two times. While taking a deep breath, touch the surface in front of you, trying to focus only on your sense of touch. Take another deep breath in and exhale, using your finger to write your empowerment slogan or a positive message to yourself on a surface in front of you.

METRONOME

Find a metronome from an online source, with a setting that is not too fast or too slow. I find 60 is a good setting, as it is one beat per second. Depending on the physical ability or processing speed, the beats per minute may need to be adjusted.

For each beat, participants will make a movement and freeze until the next beat. This can be applied as a mindful activity.

Challenge

Pause the beat, participants look at each other's paused movements. Participants can even comment if it looks like a scene has been created or if it looks like someone has created their own storyline by defining their pose.

GROUP MINDFULNESS WITH ZIP-ZAP-ZOP

Goal

- Sustaining group focus and being in the moment.

Materials

- Space to make a circle and move in.

- See following pages for pictures of *Zip-Zap-Zop* hand movements

Instructions for *Zip-Zap-Zop*

1. Form a circle.

2. The leader will demonstrate three hand movements, each associated with Zip, Zap, or Zop (see following). All hand movements direct the attention to the person you are sending the Zip, Zap, or Zop toward. Say one of the words at the same time as its hand movement is made, while directing eye contact and body toward the person you are sending the message to. (Example: Zip with hand movement to person B, then they accept it and make the next hand movement and gesture to the next person they choose, continuing the cycle.)

3. Choose one person to send the Zip movement to as they move one hand toward the receiving person with the Zip movement.

4. The receiver will then become the sender as they use the Zop movement to the person they choose to be the receiver.

5. The receiver becomes the sender as they choose to use the Zip movement to a new receiver.

6. The group will continue the pattern of Zip, Zap, and Zop hand movements and try to increase speed as time goes on and the group gains experience.

7. Repeat until all have had at least three turns.

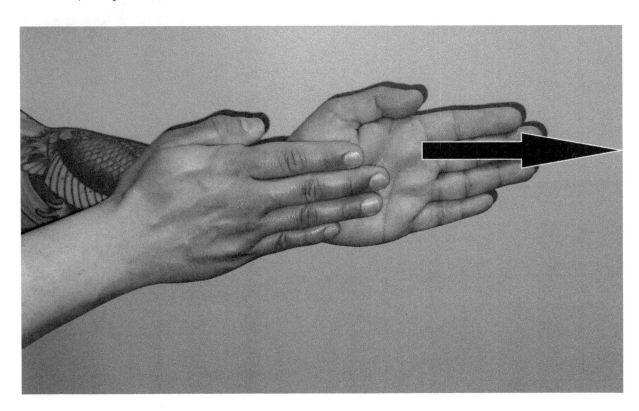

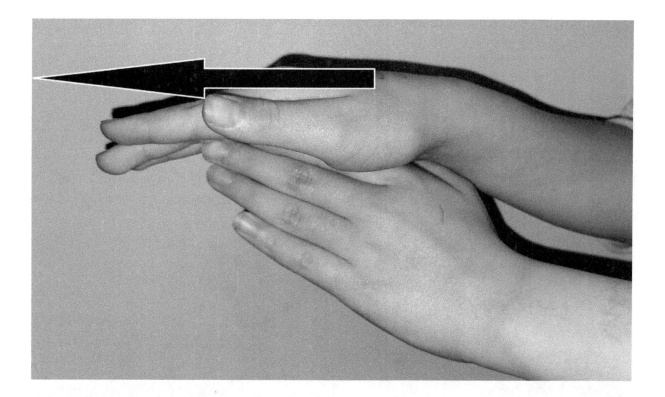

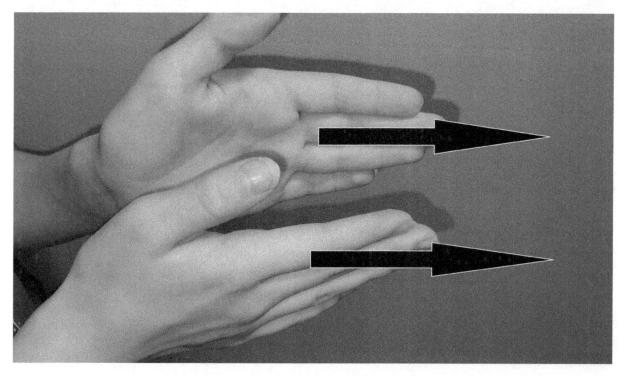

BUBBLE POP

Think of one worry or one frustration. Think about it profusely. Visualize pictures of what that worry or frustration looks like. Blow up a pretend balloon with each worry or frustration visualization. Each time you visualize another worry or frustration, imagine the picture traveling from the brain down through your breath into the balloon. Blow it up as big as needed. Then pop it, envisioning the worry or frustration popping and thus disappearing from the mind. If needed, get another balloon.

INVISIBLE SHIELD

Close your eyes and take some deep breaths. Create a shield in your mind and put an inspiring slogan on it. Imagine using your verbal shield to ward off all negative vibes, bullies, and criticism. Try holding it up against all the negative thoughts and words that have come at you. Then once it's all cleared away, put the shield behind you and walk on tall and proud. Take some deep breaths and open your eyes to the next adventure.

SUMMARY

Developing the inner monologue is an ongoing project for many in the stages of growth. It is also imperative in being more successful in social interactions and maintaining healthy self-confidence. Having good confidence leads to other positive outcomes overall. Practicing coping skills and the art of mindfulness fosters flexibility as well as confidence. Having an open mind and being positive has a ripple effect on how others view us and we view them. In turn, being more aware of the environment and surroundings you are in adds to deeper connections with people and builds self-confidence. This also leads to more successful social interactions and maintaining healthy relationships overall.

MORE DOWNLOADABLE ACTIVITIES AND MATERIALS AND EMPOWERING VOICES

For more downloadable activities, SEL-based Improv games, and worksheets visit our website at Socialtheatre.org. Moreover, if you have written a play with the Social Theatre™ model from our first book *Teaching Social Skills through Sketch Comedy and Improv Games* or have written a second scene for *I'm Stuffed!,* submit it to our website at Socialtheatre.org. We want to uplift and empower voices of students, clients, children, and all participants, and would possibly post plays with attribution to your group.

REFERENCES

Amador, S. (2018) *Teaching Social Skills through Sketch Comedy and Improv Games.* London: Jessica Kingsley Publishers.

Butterworth, G. and Jarrett, N. (1991) 'What minds have in common is space: Spatial mechanisms serving joint visual attention in infancy.' *British Journal of Developmental Psychology 9*, 1, 55–72.

CASEL (2022) 'What is the CASEL Framework?' Retrieved from https://casel.org/fundamentals-of-sel/what-is-the-casel-framework/#interactive-casel-wheel on 07/07/22.

Ching-Lin Wu, A., Lui, Y.R., Kuo, C.C., Chen, H.C., and Chang, Y.L. (2016) 'Effectiveness of humor training among adolescents with autism.' *Psychiatry Today 246*, 25–31.

Corbett, A.B., Key, A.P., Qualls, L., Fecteau, S., Newsom, C., Coke, C., and Yoder, P. (2016) 'Improvement in social competence using a randomized trial of a theatre intervention for children with autism spectrum disorder.' *Journal of Autism and Developmental Disorders 4*, 2, 658–672.

Corbett, A.B., Blain, S.D., Loannou, S., and Balser, M. (2017) 'Changes in anxiety following a randomized control trial of a theatre-based intervention for youth with autism spectrum disorder.' *Autism 21*, 3, 333–343.

DeMichelle, M. (2015) 'Improv and ink: Increasing individual writing fluency with collaborative Improv.' *International Journal of Education and the Arts 16*, 10.

DeMichelle, M. and Kuenneke, S. (2021) 'Short-form, comedy Improv affects the functional connectivity in the brain of adolescents with complex developmental trauma as measured by qEEG: A single group pilot study.' *Neuroregulation 8*, 1.

Edwards, S. (2010) 'Humor, laughter, and those aha moments'. *On The Brain 16*, Spring, 2. Retrieved from https://hms.harvard.edu/news/humor-laughter-those-aha-moments on 07/01/22.

Felsman, P., Seifert, C.M., and Himle, J.A. (2019) 'The use of improvisational theater training to reduce social anxiety in adolescents.' *The Arts in Psychotherapy 63*, 111–117.

Felsman, P., Gunawardena, S., and Seifert, C.M. (2020) 'Improv experience promotes divergent thinking, uncertainty tolerance, and affective well-being.' *Thinking Skills and Creativity 35*, 100632.

Garcia Winner, M. (2007) *Thinking About You, Thinking About Me.* San Jose, CA: Think Social Publishing.

Garcia Winner, M. (2008) *Think Social: A Social Thinking® Curriculum for School Age Students.* Santa Clara, CA: Think Social Publishing.

Garcia Winner, M. and Crook, P. (2011) *Socially Curious and Curiously Social: A Social Thinking Guidebook for Bright Teens and Young Adults.* Great Barrington, MA: North River Press.

Gernsbacher, M.A., Stevenson, J.L., Khandakar, S., and Goldsmith, H.H. (2008) 'Why does joint attention look atypical in autism?' *Child Development Perspectives 2*, 1, 38–45.

Hamid, A.A., Pettibone, J.R., Mabrouk, O.S., Hetrick, V.L., et al. (2016) 'Mesolimbic dopamine signals the value of work.' *Nature Neuroscience 19*, 117–126.

Hendrix, R., Palmer, K.Z., Tarshis, N., and Winner, M.G. (2013) *We Thinkers! Social Explorers Curriculum, Volume 1.* San Jose, CA: Think Social Publishing, Inc.

Hung, L.W., Neuner, S., Polepalli, J.S., et al. (2017) 'Gating of social reward by oxytocin in the ventral tegmental area.' *Science 357*, 6358, 1406–1411.

Koike, T., Sumiya, M., Nakagawa, E., Okazaki, S., and Sadato, N. (2019) 'What makes eye contact special? Neural substrates of on-line mutual eye-gaze: A hyperscanning fMRI study.' *eNeuro 6*, 1.

Krueger, K.R., Murphy, J.W., and Bink, A.B., (2017) 'Theraprov: A pilot study of Improv used to treat anxiety and depression.' *Journal of Mental Health 28*, 6, 621–626.

Laldin, M. (2016) 'The psychology of belonging (and why it matters).' Retrieved from www.learningandthebrain.com/blog/psychology-of-belonging on 01/22/20.

Letterman, D. (2018) 'My next guest needs no introduction: It's just landmine hopscotch.' Talk Show, May 4. New York: Netflix.

Madrigal, S. and Garcia Winner, M. (2013) *Superflex Takes on One-Sided Sid, Un-Wonderer and the Team of Unthinkables.* Santa Clara, CA: Think Social Publishing.

Porges, S. (2017) *The Pocket Guide to the Polyvagal Theory: The Transformative Power of Feeling Safe.* London: W.W. Norton and Company, Ltd.

Premack, D. and Woodruff, G. (1978) 'Does the chimpanzee have a theory of mind?' *Behavioral and Brain Sciences 4*, 4, 515–629.

Siegel, D.J. and Payne Bryson, T. (2012) *The Whole-Brain Child.* New York: Random House.

Singh Bains, G., Berk, L.S., Daher, N., Lohman, E., Schwab, E., Petrofsky, J., and Deshpande, P. (2014) 'The effect of humor on short-term memory in older adults: A new component for whole-person wellness.' *Advances in Mind-Body Medicine 28*, 2, 16–24.

Spolin, V. (1999) *Improvisation for the Theater. Third Edition.* Chicago, IL: Northwestern University Press.

van der Kolk, B.A. (2014) *The Body Keeps the Score: Brain, Mind, and Body in the Healing of Trauma.* New York: Viking.

Vera, E.M., Vacek, K., Blackmon, S., Coyle, L., et al. (2012) 'Subjective well-being in urban, ethnically diverse adolescents: The role of stress and coping.' *Youth and Society 44*, 3, 331–347.

Winner, M.G. and Crooke, P. (2020) *You Are a Social Detective! Explaining Social Thinking to Kids, 2nd Edition.* San Jose, CA: Think Social Publishing, Inc.

INDEX

SENSORY STORIES TO SUPPORT ADDITIONAL NEEDS
MAKING NARRATIVES ACCESSIBLE THROUGH THE SENSES
JOANNA GRACE

£22.99 | $32.95 | PB | 208PP | ISBN 978 1 83997 147 1 | EISBN 978 1 83997 148 8

Sensory Stories are short stories of a few lines which are brought to life through a selection of meaningful sensory experiences. They are particularly beneficial for people with Sensory Processing Disorder (SPD), Profound and Multiple Learning Difficulties (PMLD) and Autistic children or adults. Sensory stories are perfect for introducing new sensory environments in a safe, interactive way to help reduce associated anxieties and open up new avenues for communication and play.

This updated edition is packed with original ready-to-use sensory stories, including 5 additional guest sensory stories by authors from around the world and your very own story template to create a sensory experience personalized for each person. With exclusive "how to" video content and digital lesson plans, this book is the essential tool for introducing the transformative multi-sensory storytelling method into your home, classroom, or group setting.

Using everyday items and step-by-step instructions to make incorporating sensory stories accessible and simple, it has never been easier to create inclusive and fun sensory experiences to enhance the lives of those with additional needs.

Joanna Grace is a Sensory Engagement and Inclusion Specialist, doctoral researcher, author, trainer, TEDx speaker and the founder of The Sensory Projects (www.TheSensoryProjects.co.uk). Her work focuses on sharing the knowledge and creativity needed to turn inexpensive resources into effective sensory tools for inclusion.

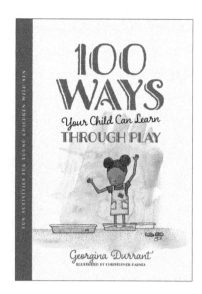

100 WAYS YOUR CHILD CAN LEARN THROUGH PLAY
FUN ACTIVITIES FOR YOUNG CHILDREN WITH SEN
GEORGINA DURRANT

£14.99 | $21.95 | PB | 128PP | ISBN 978 1 78775 734 9 | EISBN 978 1 78775 735 6

Packed full of 100 creative and engaging activities for young children with special educational needs, this book enables you to have fun and enjoy developing your child's skill-based learning with them.

From building biscuit construction sites and rainbow ice towers to playing dentists, nail salons, and post office workers, the variety and creativity featured on every page of this book means you'll never have a dull day with your child again! With activities for rainy days, in the garden, on walks and more, there's something new to learn wherever you go.

With charming black and white line illustrations to depict each activity, this is a great way to connect with your children with SEN, while building their life skills at the same time.

Georgina Durrant is a former teacher/Special Educational Needs Coordinator and is now Director of Cheshire SEN Tutor LTD. She is also a mum of 2 children under 7. Georgina runs the award-winning site The SEN Resources Blog (www.senresourcesblog.com), which provides learning activities, recommendations, resources, and advice for parents and teachers of children with Special Educational Needs.

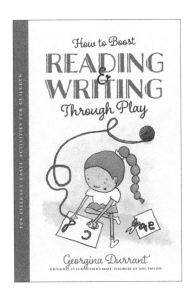

HOW TO BOOST READING AND WRITING THROUGH PLAY
FUN LITERACY-BASED ACTIVITIES FOR CHILDREN
GEORGINA DURRANT

£14.99 | $21.95 | PB | 112PP | ISBN 978 1 83997 456 4 | EISBN 978 1 83997 457 1

Even if children know their phonics and ABCs inside out and can read every book in their book bag, why is it still so difficult to get them to want to read and write? How do we begin to get our children excited about literacy? The answer might surprise you...let them play!

Featuring 40 engaging play-based activities, this book makes literacy so fun that children won't notice they're also actively developing reading and writing skills. From blow painting words to making paper chain sentences, each activity can be done using household items and they are adaptable for children of any age and ability, making learning accessible for all.

With charming black and white line illustrations to depict each activity, this is a great way to connect with children while helping to build their literacy skills at the same time.

Georgina Durrant is a former teacher/Special Educational Needs Coordinator and Director of Cheshire SEN Tutor LTD. She founded the award-winning SEN Resources Blog www.senresourcesblog.com to share activities, advice, and recommendations for parents and teachers of children with Special Educational Needs and disabilities.

THE BIG BOOK OF THERAPEUTIC ACTIVITY IDEAS FOR CHILDREN AND TEENS
INSPIRING ARTS-BASED ACTIVITIES AND CHARACTER EDUCATION
LINDSEY JOINER

£22.99 | $35 | PB | 256PP | ISBN 978 1 84905 865 0 |
EISBN 978 0 85700 447 5

For difficult or challenging children and teenagers in therapeutic or school settings, creative activities can be an excellent way of increasing enjoyment and boosting motivation, making the sessions more rewarding and successful for everyone involved.

This resource provides over one hundred tried-and-tested fun and imaginative therapeutic activities and ideas to unleash the creativity of children and teenagers from ages 5+. Employing a variety of expressive arts including art, music, stories, poetry and film, the activities are designed to teach social skills development, anger control strategies, conflict resolution and thinking skills. Also included are character education activities and ideas for conducting therapeutic day camps, including sample schedules and handouts. The activities can be used in many different settings with all ages, are flexible, and can be adapted for use with individuals or groups.

Brimming with imaginative ideas, this resource will be invaluable to anyone working with children and teenagers, including school counselors, social workers, therapists, psychologists, and teachers.

Lindsey Joiner is a Positive Behavior Specialist with Meridian Public School District in Mississippi (USA). She is a Licensed Professional Counselor, National Certified Counselor, and Board Qualified Supervisor. Many of the activities in this book were developed as part of Lindsey's experience conducting and supervising day treatment programs for children and teens in a community mental health center.

THE CBT ART ACTIVITY BOOK
100 ILLUSTRATED HANDOUTS FOR
CREATIVE THERAPEUTIC WORK
JENNIFER GUEST

£24.99 | $32.95 | PB | 136PP | ISBN 978 1 84905 665 6 | EISBN 978 1 78450 168 6

Explore complex emotions and enhance self-awareness with these 100 ready-to-use creative activities.

The intricate, attractive designs are illustrated in the popular zentangle style and are suitable for adults and young people, in individual or group work. The worksheets use cognitive behavioral therapy (CBT) and art as therapy to address outcomes including improved self-esteem, emotional wellbeing, anger management, coping with change and loss, problem solving and future planning. The coloring pages are designed for relaxing stress management and feature a complete illustrated alphabet and series of striking mandala designs.

Jennifer Guest has worked in clinical therapeutic practice as a counselor for 14 years, working with adults, couples, and young people in a variety of counseling centers and schools in the North of England. Jennifer is an Accredited Member of the British Association of Counsellors and Psychotherapists and has an honors degree in Art and Design. Currently she works for Relate, a charity that provides counseling services, and has her own private practice based in Yorkshire.